JELLY ROLL
ANIMAL QUILTS

Over 40 patterns for animal
quilts, rugs & more

Ira Rott

DAVID & CHARLES

www.davidandcharles.com

CONTENTS

PROJECTS

WELCOME!

In the world of quilting, colorful Jelly Rolls became a source of never-ending inspiration to me, and I hope they will inspire you too. These mind-blowing bundles of coordinating fabric strips are easy to use and so much fun to sew!

All quilts in this book are constructed from precut fabric strips that are sub-cut into rectangles, and then turned into 60° shapes by trimming corners in a special way.

There are 9 animal designs – a bear, an owl, a dog, a cat, a raccoon, a fox, an elephant, a ladybug and a frog – with several coordinating projects for each animal. Every project is assigned a level of difficulty, so you can start with easier patterns and move up to the next level as you get comfortable with the process.

In addition, you can mix and match blocks from different animals to create your own animal quilts. Why not make a cat and dog quilt with paw prints from the bear pattern, or use the fox and raccoon blocks for a woodland theme quilt? You can also create a cute banner for your room and a matching pillow using fabric scraps from your animal projects.

Using patterns in this book, you can make crib quilts, cuddle throw quilts, area rugs, wall hangings, pillows, mug rugs, placemats and more. The sky's the limit. I hope you enjoy making these fun animal quilts from your precut fabric strips!

Ira Rott

Happy Crafting!

HOW TO USE THIS BOOK

SKILL LEVELS

All projects in this book have been assigned a level of difficulty based on the skills required to complete them. Pick a pattern that suits your skill level, then move up to the next level as you get comfortable with the techniques.

Just Learning — Best choice for novice quilters familiar with the basics of cutting and sewing. Simple designs include small 60° units that are easy to cut and assemble. These projects are sure to get you started.

Confident Beginner — For those with basic quilting skills and confidence in learning new skills. These patterns include small and medium 60° units that are easy to assemble into larger designs.

Intermediate — For the quilters comfortable with intricate piecing and those who have a good understanding of 60° shapes. These patterns may include more complex shapes, as well as binding concave and irregular corners.

READING PATTERNS

Since precut fabric strips are manufactured using the imperial system of units, all cutting instructions and measurements are also given in inches to avoid discrepancies. Therefore, it's important to use all measuring tools accordingly to achieve accurate results.

Begin with the General Techniques section. It includes everything you need to know about cutting 60° shapes from fabric strips, as well as instructions for accurate piecing and pressing seams.

At the beginning of each of the animal projects you will find a list of materials required to complete it, both as the quantity of 2½in strips required with the yardage listed alongside. So, if you don't have precut strips, you can simply cut your own strips from fabric.

Each pattern starts with the fabric cutting instructions, arranged into lists by fabric color for convenience. The lists indicate how many fabric strips you need for cutting the shapes required, and the shapes are listed in order from longest to shortest, which helps you to arrange the most efficient cutting layout.

The materials list also includes any additional pieces to be cut from fabric yardage. These are indicated by the "+" symbol, and are for areas such as borders or filler blocks.

Once you have cut out all of the shapes, assemble them according to the pattern and diagram descriptions.

Quilting diagrams are essential for visualizing patterns. They show fabric colors and shapes that need to be sewn together. Some diagrams have red arrows to indicate the joining of units or of single shapes in a specific order.

If you are not familiar with quilting terminology, be sure to check out the Useful Information section, where you can also find instructions on many other useful topics including: measuring and sewing quilt borders; making a quilt sandwich; binding techniques for a variety of shaped projects; finishing quilts without binding; and general tips for quilting.

PROJECTS

Each animal design chapter includes several coordinating projects, such as area rugs, wall hangings, quilts, placemats and mug rugs. Pick just one or make them all for a complete set. Wall hangings are like area rugs, but have a background and are rectangular in shape. They can be used to decorate walls or as play mats. The wall hanging animal blocks are incorporated into larger quilts. In addition, you can use fabric leftovers to make units or blocks from the main projects to create the extras suggested at the end of each chapter, including fun banners and practical pillows, (see Additional Ideas for general advice on project construction).

In the Additional Ideas section, you'll also find useful tips for mixing different animals into one quilt, creating an improvised backing, upcycling old jeans for stunning backgrounds, finishing a wall hanging and adding a non-slip backing to your area rugs.

TOOLS AND MATERIALS

FABRICS

PRECUT STRIPS

Jelly Rolls are bundles of precut fabric strips, invented by Moda Fabrics in 2006. They are now also known as Design Rolls, Roll-Ups, Rolie Polies, Pinwheels, Strip Packs and Strip Sets by different fabric brands. These beautiful bundles of fabric usually include 40–42 precut fabric strips that are 2½in wide and 42–44in long. With a wide variety of coordinating colors and prints in one package, these strips are perfect for making the quilts in this book.

FABRIC BY THE YARD

Only excellent fabrics can create excellent quilts. When it comes to fabric options, medium-weight quilting cotton is the best choice for making quilts. Quilting cotton is a tightly woven 100% cotton fabric, which is heavier than apparel cotton due to higher thread counts. Batiks are also great for quilting as they are made with a higher thread count.

Fabric by the yard should be at least 42in wide. It can be used for backings, backgrounds, binding and even cutting your own strip bundles.

For the projects in this book, I used Patrick Lose and Northcott fabrics, the home of "cottons that feel like silk".

THREAD

When considering your thread options, it's important to choose the correct weight, color and fiber content. I used Aurifil 50wt cotton thread for all projects in this book.

Weight – The weight is the thickness of thread, indicated by the number. The higher the number, the thinner the thread; the lower the number, the thicker the thread. Your thread weight should always match the size of your needle and the thickness of fabric. A 50wt thread is perfect for piecing, quilting and binding. If you want your quilting stitches to stand out more, you can use 40wt thread for quilting.

Color – The color of your thread should match the fabric as closely as possible. When the exact color is not available, or using multiple colors is not an option, you can choose a neutral-colored thread for piecing, and a color that blends with the fabrics in your quilt for quilting. A lighter thread is often a better choice than darker thread. You can also use variegated thread for quilting.

Fiber – Ideally, the fiber content of the thread should match the fabric. Therefore, 100% cotton thread is a good choice for cotton fabric. However, polyester threads are safe for piecing and quilting as well, and they won't damage your fabrics.

BATTING

Batting is a layer of soft fibers used as insulation between two layers of fabric. You can use 100% cotton batting or an 80/20% cotton-polyester blend, and both are wonderful options, but don't use 100% polyester batting as some projects are pressed with a hot iron. All quilts in this book are made using Hobbs Heirloom 80/20% cotton-polyester batting as it offers more loft and less weight than traditional cotton batting. Other small projects will perform well with 100% natural cotton batting.

SEWING MACHINE

A domestic sewing machine is perfect for piecing and quilting. You do not need anything special, but some features can make the process easier. For instance, a larger throat space will help you move fabrics more easily while quilting. Also, a straight stitch needle plate will prevent the leading edge from puckering while piecing.

NOTIONS

CUTTING TOOLS

- 24 x 36in self healing cutting mat for most of your cutting needs
- 12 x 12in rotating self healing cutting mat for convenience in cutting 60° shapes (optional)
- Rotary cutter with a 45mm blade
- Fabric scissors for cutting fabrics and batting
- Fabric snips for notching and clipping corners
- Thread snips or scissors for cutting thread
- Paper scissors for cutting templates
- Seam ripper for fixing mistakes

RULERS

- Quilting ruler 6 x 24in for cutting long strips and borders
- Quilting ruler 6 x 12in for cutting smaller shapes
- 60° corner trimmer or 60° ruler with trimmed corners for cutting 60° shapes; you can also use a paper template along with a regular quilting ruler (see General Techniques)
- Curved corner cutter (3in radius) for creating round corners on some of the animal rugs (a small round plate is a good alternative)

OTHER

- Bias tape maker
- Steam iron for pressing seams
- Ironing board or pressing mat

GENERAL TECHNIQUES

GETTING STARTED

Take the time to sort your 2½in strips from the pack to ensure that you have the right number for each color section. Focus on overall appearance, coordinating color schemes and values (light, medium and dark). For example, all the strips for fabric A do not have to be identical (although they can be), but you may group different prints with similar values and colors. It's good practice to reserve an extra strip to cover mistakes if they happen, and to refer to the quilting diagrams when planning your cutting.

Ensure there is a clear distinction between the animal and the background fabric in quilts or wall hangings to prevent color blending. For instance, use colorful fabric strips for the animals, and choose a neutral colored fabric for the background (lighter or darker in value). In my projects, I like to use small non-directional prints, tone-on-tone prints, stripes and solids.

DEFINITION OF SHAPES

Let's start by looking in detail at the shapes required for the piecing of the animal designs before moving on to review how to cut these shapes in detail.

	Rectangle – A quadrilateral (four-sided shape) with four right angles in which the opposite sides are parallel and equal to each other. You will be cutting rectangles from 2½in strips using a regular quilting ruler.
	Equilateral Triangle – A triangle in which all three sides are equal and all the angles are 60°. You will be cutting triangles from 2½in strips using a 60° corner trimmer.
	Isosceles Trapezoid – A quadrilateral with one pair of parallel sides, and two nonparallel sides equal in length. You will be sub-cutting 2½in strips into rectangles and then trimming corners in a special way using a 60° corner trimmer.
	Right-angled Trapezoid – A trapezoid with two right angles and one acute angle. The left-leaning trapezoid has its acute angle leaning to the left (L), and the right-leaning trapezoid has its acute angle leaning to the right (R). You will be sub-cutting 2½in strips into rectangles and then trimming corners in a special way with a 60° corner trimmer.
	Parallelogram – A quadrilateral with two pairs of parallel sides. The left-leaning parallelogram has its short sides leaning to the left (L), and the right-leaning parallelogram has its short sides leaning to the right (R). You will be sub-cutting 2½in strips into rectangles and then trimming corners in a special way with a 60° corner trimmer.

CUTTING STRIPS

If your strip pack does not have a certain color, you can cut your own strips from fabric. Simply fold fabric in half, holding selvages together and parallel to the folded edge. Square up the left edge if you are right-handed or right edge if you are left-handed. Lay the 24in ruler on top of the fabric, measuring 2½in from the edge. Make the cut and repeat as needed **(1)**.

CUTTING SHAPES

Begin by sub-cutting 2½in strips into rectangles to the specified length. The length of these rectangles is precisely calculated and is rounded to the closest ¼in mark for simplicity in cutting. To create 60° shapes, trim the corners off of the rectangles using a 60° corner trimmer or a ruler with trimmed 60° corners (see Cutting Steps). It's important not to use the 60° markings on a regular quilting ruler or a ruler with pointy 60° corners. If the point of a ruler meets the corner, you will trim off the seam allowance and your shape will be too short. If you do not have a special ruler, you can trace or print the 60° Corner Trimmer Template provided and use it along with a regular quilting ruler (see Using Paper Templates).

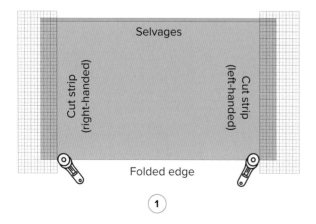

1

HANDY TIPS

For accuracy, when working with precuts, carefully ensure that the width of your strips measure exactly 2½in, especially if the strips have pinked edges. If the strip is wider, you can trim off any excess before cutting shapes. If the strip is narrower, you can sew those sides with a scant ¼in seam allowance.

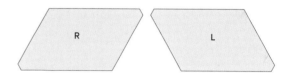

To cut symmetrical shapes, place two strips with wrong sides together and cut as one.

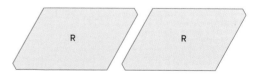

To cut identical shapes, place two or more strips with right sides facing the same direction and cut as one.

Note: Equilateral triangles and isosceles trapezoids can be cut with multiple layers of fabrics facing either direction.

CUTTING STEPS

SHAPES	STEP 1	STEP 2	FINISHED
Rectangle			
Equilateral Triangle			
Isosceles Trapezoid			
Right-leaning Trapezoid			
Left-leaning Trapezoid			
Right-leaning Parallelogram			
Left-leaning Parallelogram			

Cut

Discards

Quilting Ruler

Corner Trimmer

USiNG PAPER TEMPLATES

As an alternative to the acrylic corner trimmer, you can trace or print the 60° Corner Trimmer Template provided. Prepare two templates using one of the following methods. Note: you will be using one template for trimming sides and the other template for trimming corners.

Tracing Templates — Position a transparent piece of paper over the template **(2)** and tape it in place using masking tape. Trace all the lines (including the dashed lines) using a ruler and a sharp pencil. Remove masking tape and trace a second time in the same manner.

Printing Templates — Open the template page using the link provided **(2)** and follow the instructions on printing it correctly.

Using Templates — Cut out your two templates precisely using paper scissors. Position the first template behind your quilting ruler, aligning the side edge of the triangle with the ruler edge and the dashed line with the ¼in mark on your ruler; tape the template to the ruler. Position the second template on the back side of the same ruler or to another quilting ruler, aligning the trimmed corner with the edge of the ruler and the corner of the dashed line with the ¼in mark on your ruler; tape the template to the ruler.

Cut the sides of the shapes by using the first template and ruler **(3–4)**, then trim the corners by using the second template and ruler **(5)**.

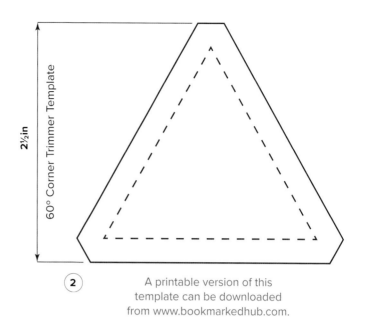

2½in

60° Corner Trimmer Template

2

A printable version of this template can be downloaded from www.bookmarkedhub.com.

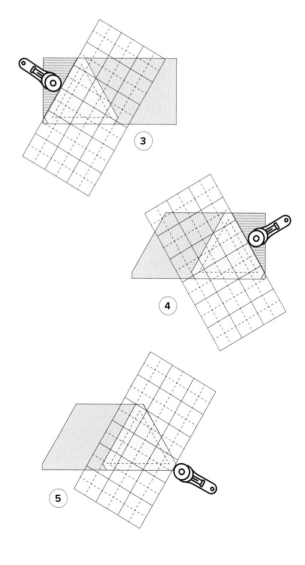

3

4

5

LABELING SHAPES

Label the shapes as you cut them to keep all your pieces in order. To make labels, you can use masking tape, small sticky labels, or paper and pins. The following is a brief explanation of what the label abbreviations mean in the patterns.

LETTERS AT THE BEGINNING

These indicate the color of fabric (A, B, C, etc.). Double letters (BB) are used for right and left-leaning trapezoids to distinguish them from parallelograms (B).

NUMBERS

These indicate the area of 60° shapes (the larger the number, the longer the shape). For instance, 1 is always an equilateral triangle, 2 is a parallelogram with the area equal to two triangles, 3 is an isosceles trapezoid with the area equal to three triangles, and so on. All parallelograms have even numbers and all isosceles trapezoids have odd numbers.

Right-angled trapezoids are cut from the same rectangles as parallelograms and isosceles trapezoids.

| 6½in | If rectangles are cut from Jelly Roll strips and are used in the pattern without shaping corners, they are indicated by the length of these rectangles in inches. |

LETTERS AT THE END

These indicate a left (L) or right (R) leaning appearance in parallelograms and right-angled trapezoids. These letters do not apply to isosceles trapezoids and equilateral triangles as they are symmetrical shapes, which means their left and right corners are mirrored.

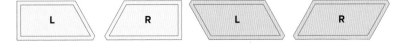

PIECING

A true ¼in seam allowance is crucial for accurate piecing. Therefore, use a patchwork presser foot on your sewing machine and check your seams for accuracy.

Shorten your stitch length for piecing to 1.5–1.6mm. The straight stitch needle plate is a bonus if you have it, as it prevents the leading edge from puckering when you start piecing. If you do not have the straight stitch needle plate, you can use a small piece of fabric as a leader to help you start sewing. Where possible, use a chain-piecing method to increase speed and efficiency, sewing unit after unit without cutting thread in between each set. To avoid distortion when sewing larger shapes, pin fabrics between the aligned edges and adjoining points.

When you sew 60° shapes together, the corners will align perfectly without dog-ears, so there will be no points that stick out past the seam allowance **(6)**. If the shapes have 60° / 120° corners on each side, pin and sew from corner to corner by distributing fabric layers evenly **(7)**; never trim the sides. However, when piecing the right and left-leaning trapezoids, always align their 60° / 120° corners and sew to the side with the right angles **(8)**; don't worry if the sides with the right angles do not match up perfectly as they will be trimmed. If larger units have right-angled trapezoids on one or both sides, match and pin all intersecting points instead of matching sides with 90° corners; these sides will be squared up later **(9)**.

PRESSING

For accuracy, set the seams before pressing, then press all seams open as you sew **(10)**, unless otherwise indicated. If you are making an area rug without a background and there are units where one piece is longer than the other, these seams need to be pressed to the side of the shorter piece **(11)**. You can also press to the side if it helps you reduce bulk in seams, for example, when working with denim strips (see Additional Ideas).

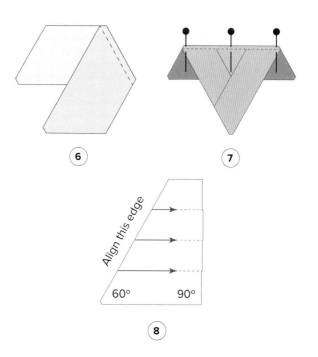

6   7

Align this edge

60°   90°

8

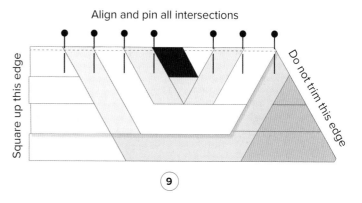

Align and pin all intersections

Square up this edge

Do not trim this edge

9

10

11

CUDDLY BEAR

The cuddly bear quilt is so lovable and huggable, it will make you want to hibernate. Whip up a matching mug rug for your morning beverage so you can stay under the quilt a little longer. An adorable area rug and a wall hanging will make great additions to a bear-themed nursery or bedroom, or even your craft room! Cozy pillows and a cute banner are quick to make using fabric leftovers and are ideal for beginners.

This theme features Northcott Stonehenge Gradations Strip Pack (Iron Ore) and Stonehenge Gradations fabrics for bear paws, background and backing. Piecing and quilting are done using Aurifil 50wt cotton thread in coordinating colors.

Color Key

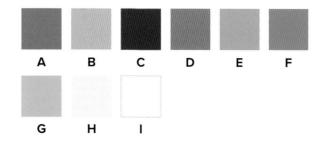

A   B   C   D   E   F

G   H   I

AREA RUG

Materials

A: 9 medium brown strips (2½in x WOF) or ¾yd

B: 3 light brown strips (2½in x WOF) or ¼yd

C: 1 dark brown strip (2½in x WOF) or fabric scraps

I: 1 white strip (2½in x WOF) or fabric scraps

Backing: 1yd

Binding: ½yd of fabric or 130in of 2½in bias binding strip

Finished Size

32 x 26in

CUTTING FABRICS

A Use 9 medium brown strips (2½in x WOF)

A19 Cut 1 piece: 2½ x 23¾in; trim to create an isosceles trapezoid.

A15 Cut 2 pieces: 2½ x 19in; trim to create isosceles trapezoids.

A13 Cut 2 pieces: 2½ x 16¾in; trim to create isosceles trapezoids.

A11 Cut 1 piece: 2½ x 14½in; trim to create an isosceles trapezoid.

AA7R & AA7L Cut 2 pieces: 2½ x 9¾in; trim to create 1 right-leaning trapezoid and 1 left-leaning trapezoid.

AA6R & AA6L Cut 2 pieces: 2½ x 8¾in; trim to create 1 right-leaning trapezoid and 1 left-leaning trapezoid.

A6R & A6L Cut 4 pieces: 2½ x 8¾in; trim to create 2 right-leaning parallelograms and 2 left-leaning parallelograms.

A4R & A4L Cut 12 pieces: 2½ x 6½in; trim to create 6 right-leaning parallelograms and 6 left-leaning parallelograms.

AA3R & AA3L Cut 4 pieces: 2½ x 5¼in; trim to create 2 right-leaning trapezoids and 2 left-leaning trapezoids.

A2R & A2L Cut 2 pieces: 2½ x 4in; trim to create 1 right-leaning parallelogram and 1 left-leaning parallelogram.

A1 Cut 4 equilateral triangles.

B Use 3 light brown strips (2½in x WOF)

B7 Cut 1 piece: 2½ x 9¾in; trim to create an isosceles trapezoid.

B5 Cut 3 pieces: 2½ x 7½in; trim to create isosceles trapezoids.

B4R & B4L Cut 2 pieces: 2½ x 6½in; trim to create 1 right-leaning parallelogram and 1 left-leaning parallelogram.

B3 Cut 8 pieces: 2½ x 5¼in; trim to create isosceles trapezoids.

B1 Cut 2 equilateral triangles.

C Use 1 dark brown strip (2½in x WOF)

C3 Cut 3 pieces: 2½ x 5¼in; trim to create isosceles trapezoids.

C2R Cut 2 pieces: 2½ x 4in; trim to create 2 right-leaning parallelograms.

I Use 1 white strip (2½in x WOF)

I1 Cut 2 equilateral triangles.

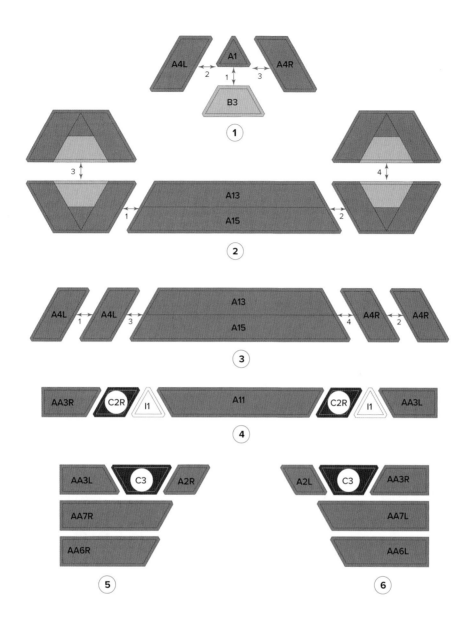

PIECING AND QUILTING

Sew with a ¼in seam allowance, pressing the seams open unless otherwise indicated.

HEAD CROWN AND EARS
Construct 4 half-ear units – Sew B3, A1, A4R and A4L together in the order indicated **(1)**.

Construct 1 crown unit – Sew A13 and A15 together **(2)**. Sew the crown unit and 4 half-ear units together in the order indicated, pressing the seams to the shorter sides in steps 3 and 4 **(2)**.

FOREHEAD
Sew A13 and A15 together **(3)**. Sew 2 pieces A4L and 2 pieces A4R to the unit just made in the order indicated **(3)**.

TOP EYES
Sew A11, AA3R, AA3L, 2 pieces C2R and 2 pieces I1 together **(4)**.

BOTTOM EYES
When sewing rows, align the 60° / 120° corners and sew to the side with the right angles. Don't worry if the sides with right angles do not match up perfectly as they will be trimmed later.

Construct the left-facing eye unit – Sew AA3L, C3 and A2R together, then sew AA7R and AA6R to the bottom of the unit just made **(5)**.

Construct the right-facing eye unit – Sew AA3R, C3 and A2L together, then sew AA7L and AA6L to the bottom of the unit just made **(6)**.

MUZZLE

Sew C3, 2 pieces B5, 4 pieces B3 and 2 pieces B1 together in the order indicated **(7)**.

FACE

Sew the muzzle, top eyes and bottom eyes together in the order indicated **(8)**. In step 3, align the intersecting points of the eyes using pins – don't worry about matching up the side edges. Once finished, square up the sides.

CHIN

Sew B5, B7, B4R, B4L, A19, 2 pieces A6L and 2 pieces A6R together in the order indicated **(9)**.

FINAL ASSEMBLY

Sew all the units together in the order indicated **(10)**. In step 1, align the sides of the forehead unit with the center points of the ears; pin and sew, then press the seam to the shorter side.

QUILTING AND BINDING

Make a quilt sandwich and quilt it as you like (see Useful Information). Trim away the excess batting and backing around the edges. Using a ruler with curved edges or a round plate, round up all the points around the head **(10)**. Prepare a bias binding, 130in in length (see Useful Information: Bias Binding). Bind your rug (see Useful Information: Binding Quilts With Curved Edges). Add a non-slip backing if desired (see Additional Ideas).

A non-slip backing cut from a rug pad material will prevent your rug from sliding on a slippery floor.

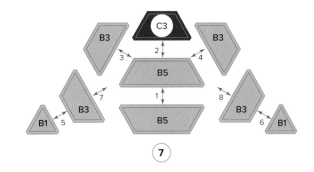

(7)

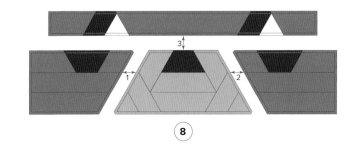

(8)

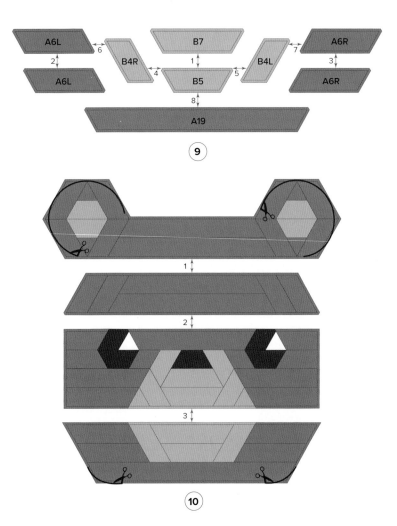

(9)

(10)

WALL HANGING

Materials

A: 9 medium brown strips (2½in x WOF) or ¾yd

B: 3 light brown strips (2½in x WOF) or ¼yd

C: 1 dark brown strip (2½in x WOF) or fabric scraps

H: 5 light neutral strips (2½in x WOF) or ½yd

I: 1 white strip (2½in x WOF) or fabric scraps

Backing: 1yd

Binding: 4 strips (2½in x WOF) or ½yd

Finished Size

37 x 26in

CUTTING FABRICS

Cut the shapes from fabrics A, B, C and I as described for the Area Rug, then cut the background pieces from fabric H as follows.

H Use 5 light neutral strips (2½in x WOF)

H15 Cut 1 piece: 2½ x 19in; trim to create an isosceles trapezoid.

H13 Cut 1 piece: 2½ x 16¾in; trim to create an isosceles trapezoid.

HH6R & HH6L Cut 2 pieces: 2½ x 8¾in; trim to create 1 right-leaning trapezoid and 1 left-leaning trapezoid.

HH5R & HH5L Cut 4 pieces: 2½ x 7½in; trim to create 2 right-leaning trapezoids and 2 left-leaning trapezoids.

HH4R & HH4L Cut 4 pieces: 2½ x 6½in; trim to create 2 right-leaning trapezoids and 2 left-leaning trapezoids.

HH3R & HH3L Cut 4 pieces: 2½ x 5¼in; trim to create 2 right-leaning trapezoids and 2 left-leaning trapezoids.

H-5¼in Cut 8 pieces: 2½ x 5¼in.

HH2R & HH2L Cut 4 pieces: 2½ x 4in; trim to create 2 right-leaning trapezoids and 2 left-leaning trapezoids.

The instructions for the wall hanging use the same color arrangement as the area rug and the quilt, but you could explore incorporating complementary colors, as seen here. Playing with colors is always fun!

PIECING AND QUILTING

Sew with a ¼in seam allowance, pressing the seams open.

HEAD CROWN AND EARS

Construct 4 half-ear units – Same as for the Area Rug **(1)**.

Construct 1 crown unit – Sew A13 and A15 together **(11)**.

Construct the background pieces – Sew H13 and H15 together, sew HH3R and HH2R together twice, sew HH3L and HH2L together twice **(11)**. Sew the crown unit, 4 half-ear units and background units together in the order indicated **(11)**.

FOREHEAD, FACE AND CHIN

Same as for the Area Rug **(3–9)**.

FINAL ASSEMBLY

In the following instructions, when piecing the right and left-leaning trapezoids, always align their 60° / 120° corners and sew to the side with the right angles.

Construct the background units – Sew HH4R and HH5R together; sew HH4L and HH5L together; sew HH4R, HH5R and HH6R together; sew HH4L, HH5L and HH6L together; sew 4 pieces H-5¼in together twice **(12)**.

Sew all the units together in the order indicated **(12)**. When sewing rows (steps 7–9), align all intersecting points using pins and do not worry about matching up the side edges. Square up the finished top.

QUILTING AND BINDING

Make a quilt sandwich and quilt it as you like (see Useful Information). Bind your wall hanging using 4 strips 2½in x WOF (see Useful Information: Binding Rectangular Quilts). Add a few picture hanging strips to display the finished piece on the wall (see Additional Ideas: Wall Hanging).

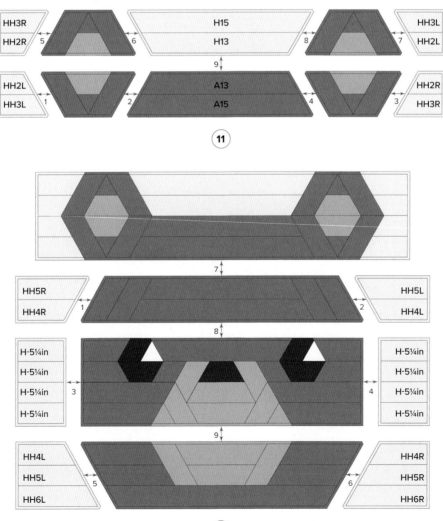

QuiLt

Materials

A: 20 medium brown strips (2½in x WOF) or 1½yd

B: 6 light brown strips (2½in x WOF) or ½yd

C: 2 dark brown strips (2½in x WOF) or ¼yd

D: 1 dark orange strip (2½in x WOF) or fabric scraps

E: 3 light orange strips (2½in x WOF) or ¼yd

F: 1 dark aqua strip (2½in x WOF) or fabric scraps

G: 3 light aqua strips (2½in x WOF) or ¼yd

H: 21 light neutral strips (2½in x WOF) + 1¼yd or 3yd in total

I: 1 white strip (2½in x WOF) or fabric scraps

Backing: 4½yd

Binding: 7 strips (2½in x WOF) or ¾yd

Finished Size

61 x 70in

CUTTING FABRICS

Make 2 bear blocks as described for the Wall Hanging, then cut the additional pieces as follows.

A Use 2 medium brown strips (2½in x WOF)

A-21½in Cut 2 pieces: 2½ x 21½in.

D Use 1 dark orange strip (2½in x WOF)

D5 Cut 4 pieces: 2½ x 7½in; trim to create isosceles trapezoids.
D3 Cut 2 pieces: 2½ x 5¼in; trim to create isosceles trapezoids.

E Use 3 light orange strips (2½in x WOF)

E7 Cut 2 pieces: 2½ x 9¾in; trim to create isosceles trapezoids.
E4R & E4L Cut 4 pieces: 2½ x 6½in; trim to create 2 right-leaning parallelograms and 2 left-leaning parallelograms.
E3 Cut 8 pieces: 2½ x 5¼in; trim to create isosceles trapezoids.

F Use 1 dark aqua strip (2½in x WOF)

F5 Cut 4 pieces: 2½ x 7½in; trim to create isosceles trapezoids.
F3 Cut 2 pieces: 2½ x 5¼in; trim to create isosceles trapezoids.

G Use 3 light aqua strips (2½in x WOF)

G7 Cut 2 pieces: 2½ x 9¾in; trim to create isosceles trapezoids.
G4R & G4L Cut 4 pieces: 2½ x 6½in; trim to create 2 right-leaning parallelograms and 2 left-leaning parallelograms.
G3 Cut 8 pieces: 2½ x 5¼in; trim to create isosceles trapezoids.

H Use 11 light neutral strips (2½in x WOF)

HH10R & HH10L Cut 4 pieces: 2½ x 13¼in; trim to create 2 right-leaning trapezoids and 2 left-leaning trapezoids.

HH9R & HH9L Cut 8 pieces: 2½ x 12¼in; trim to create 4 right-leaning trapezoids and 4 left-leaning trapezoids.

HH7R & HH7L Cut 8 pieces: 2½ x 9¾in; trim to create 4 right-leaning trapezoids and 4 left-leaning trapezoids.

H-8¾in Cut 4 pieces: 2½ x 8¾in.

HH5R & HH5L Cut 4 pieces: 2½ x 7½in; trim to create 2 right-leaning trapezoids and 2 left-leaning trapezoids.

HH4R & HH4L Cut 8 pieces: 2½ x 6½in; trim to create 4 right-leaning trapezoids and 4 left-leaning trapezoids.

HH2R & HH2L Cut 8 pieces: 2½ x 4in; trim to create 4 right-leaning trapezoids and 4 left-leaning trapezoids.

H1 Cut 4 equilateral triangles.

H Use additional light neutral fabric (1¼yd)

Cut away selvages, then cut the following border pieces:

Bear Block Borders Cut 3 strips 5in x WOF.

Paw Block Borders Cut 2 strips 4½in x LOF; cut 1 strip 5in x LOF; cut 2 strips 9in x LOF.

PIECING AND QUILTING

Sew with a ¼in seam allowance unless otherwise indicated, pressing the seams open.

PAW BLOCKS

Construct 2 orange paw blocks **(13)** – Sew HH4R, 2 pieces E3, H1 and HH9L together (Row 1); sew HH4L, E7 and HH9R together (Row 2); sew HH2R, E4R, D3, E4L and HH7L together (Row 3); sew HH2L, 2 pieces E3, D5 and HH7R together (Row 4); sew HH5L, D5 and HH10R together (Row 5). Sew these 5 rows together. When sewing rows, align all intersecting points using pins and do not worry about matching up the side edges. Square up the finished block.

Construct 2 aqua paw blocks **(14)** – Sew HH9R, 2 pieces G3, H1 and HH4L together (Row 1); sew HH9L, G7 and HH4R together (Row 2); sew HH7R, G4R, F3, G4L and HH2L together (Row 3); sew HH7L, 2 pieces G3, F5 and HH2R together (Row 4); sew HH10L, F5 and HH5R together (Row 5). Sew these 5 rows together in the same manner as for the orange paw block. Square up the finished block.

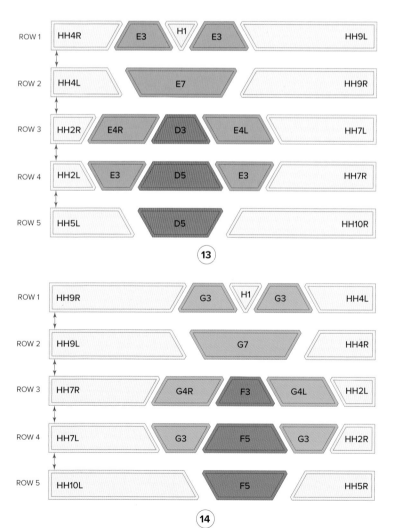

BEAR NECK

Construct 2 units – Sew 2 pieces H-8¾in and A-21½in together **(15)**.

FINAL ASSEMBLY

Referring to Useful Information: Borders, trim the edges of the 3 bear block borders and 2 bear neck units to the width of your bear blocks; trim the edges of all paw block borders to the width of your paw blocks. Sew all the pieces together in the order indicated **(16)**.

QUILTING AND BINDING

Cut the backing fabric in half across WOF. Cut away selvages and sew 2 pieces together along the long sides with a ½in seam allowance; press the seam open. Make a quilt sandwich and quilt it as you like (see Useful Information). Bind your quilt using 7 strips 2½in x WOF (see Useful Information: Binding Rectangular Quilts).

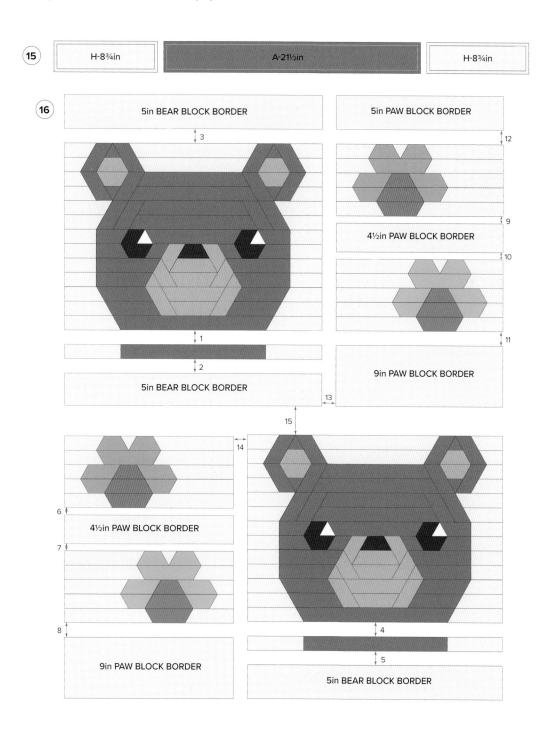

MUG RUG

Materials

D / F: 1 dark orange or dark aqua strip (2½in x WOF) or fabric scraps

E / G: 3 light orange or light aqua strips (2½in x WOF) or ¼yd

Backing: 16 x 12in

Finished Size

14 x 10in

CUTTING FABRICS

Cut the shapes from fabrics D and E (orange) as shown in the diagrams, (or from aqua fabrics F and G if you prefer), as described for the Quilt.

PIECING AND QUILTING

Sew with a ¼in seam allowance, pressing the seams open unless otherwise indicated.

FINAL ASSEMBLY AND QUILTING

Cut away the ¼in seam allowances on the mirrored edges of 2 of the E3 pieces **(17)**. Sew these pieces to the longest edge of E7 **(18)**. The trimmed edges should be overlapping each other by ¼in in the center. Sew the remaining pieces in the order indicated, pressing the seams to the shorter sides in steps 6 and 7 **(19)**.

Finish your mug rug without binding and quilt it as you like (see Useful Information: Rug Without Binding).

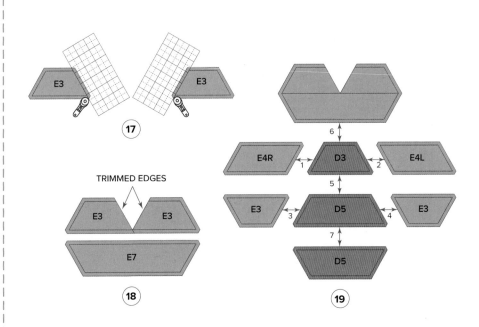

EXTRAS

PILLOWCASE

To make a square pillowcase approx. 18 x 18in, you will need 1 dark and 2 light strips for the paw, 4 background strips of your choosing, plus fabrics for backing and binding. Make a paw block by using the background shapes from the left side of diagram **(13)** and the right side of diagram **(14)**. Add 2 background strips to the top and 2 to the bottom edges to make it square, then finish your pillowcase as described in Additional Ideas: Pillowcase.

BANNER

You will need 2 dark and 4 light strips of orange and aqua plus fabrics for backing and binding. From strips D, E, F and G, construct 5–6 flag units referring to the ear units from the bear block in the Area Rug **(1–2)**. Cut parallelograms from the darker fabrics and use lighter fabrics for trapezoids and triangles. Each finished flag measures 8in vertically and 9in horizontally, so you can estimate the length for your banner. Finish the banner as described in Additional Ideas: Banner.

SPARKLY OWL

Stay warm at night and sleep tight with this sparkly owl quilt. If glitter is your favorite color, choose a bundle of sparkling fabric strips from your collection and add some coordinating fabrics. A good quality thread and natural soft batting are also wise ideas. Optionally, make an area rug or a lovely wall hanging. Save leftovers from the colorful fabric strips to create a fun banner for your room in the blink of an eye.

This theme features Northcott Shimmer Strip Pack (Midnight Sky) along with the Shimmer Single Colorway and Shimmer Radiance Single Colorway. Piecing and quilting are done using Aurifil 50wt cotton thread in coordinating colors.

Color key

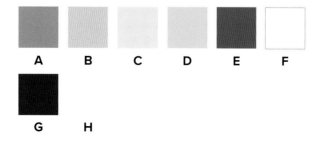

A	B	C	D	E	F

G	H

AREA RUG

Materials

A: 4–5 dark purple strips (2½in x WOF) or ½yd

B: 4 light purple strips (2½in x WOF) or ½yd

C: 2 light blue strips (2½in x WOF) or ¼yd

D: 2 medium green strips (2½in x WOF) or ¼yd

E: 4 medium blue strips (2½in x WOF) or ½yd

F: 3 white strips (2½in x WOF) or ¼yd

G: 1 dark blue strip (2½in x WOF) or fabric scraps

Backing: 1¼yd

Finished Size

41 x 34in

CUTTING FABRICS

A Use 4–5 dark purple strips (2½in x WOF)

A9 Cut 7 pieces: 2½ x 12¼in; trim to create isosceles trapezoids.

A8R & A8L Cut 4 pieces: 2½ x 11in; trim to create 2 right-leaning parallelograms and 2 left-leaning parallelograms.

A4R & A4L Cut 2 pieces: 2½ x 6½in; trim to create 1 right-leaning parallelogram and 1 left-leaning parallelogram.

A1 Cut 6 equilateral triangles.

B Use 4 light purple strips (2½in x WOF)

B15 Cut 2 pieces: 2½ x 19in; trim to create isosceles trapezoids.

B13 Cut 2 pieces: 2½ x 16¾in; trim to create isosceles trapezoids.

B11 Cut 1 piece: 2½ x 14½in; trim to create an isosceles trapezoid.

B9 Cut 1 piece: 2½ x 12¼in; trim to create an isosceles trapezoid.

B5 Cut 2 pieces: 2½ x 7½in; trim to create isosceles trapezoids.

B3 Cut 2 pieces: 2½ x 5¼in; trim to create isosceles trapezoids.

B1 Cut 2 equilateral triangles.

C Use 2 light blue strips (2½in x WOF)

C9 Cut 2 pieces: 2½ x 12¼in; trim to create isosceles trapezoids.

C6R & C6L Cut 4 pieces: 2½ x 8¾in; trim to create 2 right-leaning parallelograms and 2 left-leaning parallelograms.

C5 Cut 2 pieces: 2½ x 7½in; trim to create isosceles trapezoids.

D Use 2 medium green strips (2½in x WOF)

D4R & D4L Cut 8 pieces: 2½ x 6½in; trim to create 4 right-leaning parallelograms and 4 left-leaning parallelograms.

D1 Cut 4 equilateral triangles.

E Use 4 medium blue strips (2½in x WOF)

E13 Cut 1 piece: 2½ x 16¾in; trim to create an isosceles trapezoid.

E11 Cut 1 piece: 2½ x 14½in; trim to create an isosceles trapezoid.

E10R & E10L Cut 2 pieces: 2½ x 13¼in; trim to create 1 right-leaning parallelogram and 1 left-leaning parallelogram.

E5 Cut 10 pieces: 2½ x 7½in; trim to create isosceles trapezoids.

E4R & E4L Cut 2 pieces: 2½ x 6½in; trim to create 1 right-leaning parallelogram and 1 left-leaning parallelogram.

E3 Cut 1 piece: 2½ x 5¼in; trim to create an isosceles trapezoid.

E1 Cut 1 equilateral triangle.

F Use 3 white strips (2½in x WOF)

F7 Cut 4 pieces: 2½ x 9¾in; trim to create isosceles trapezoids.

F4R & F4L Cut 8 pieces: 2½ x 6½in; trim to create 4 right-leaning parallelograms and 4 left-leaning parallelograms.

F1 Cut 2 equilateral triangles.

G Use 1 dark blue strip (2½in x WOF)

G3 Cut 2 pieces: 2½ x 5¼in; trim to create isosceles trapezoids.

G2R Cut 2 pieces: 2½ x 4in; trim to create 2 right-leaning parallelograms.

G1 Cut 6 equilateral triangles.

PIECING AND QUILTING

Sew with a ¼in seam allowance, pressing the seams open unless otherwise indicated.

EYEBROWS
Construct the left-leaning eyebrow – Sew E4R and 4 pieces E5 together with bottom-alignment, pressing the seams to the shorter side; sew E10L to the bottom of the unit just made **(1)**.

Construct the right-leaning eyebrow – Sew E4L and 4 pieces E5 together with bottom-alignment, pressing the seams to the shorter side; sew E10R to the bottom of the unit just made **(2)**.

BEAK
Sew E1, E3, 2 pieces E5 and 2 pieces A1 together in the order indicated **(3)**. Sew A9, E11 and E13 to the unit just made in the order indicated **(4)**.

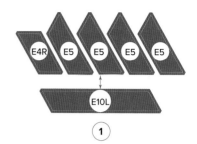

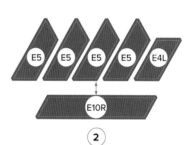

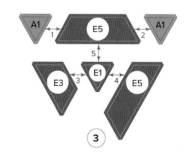

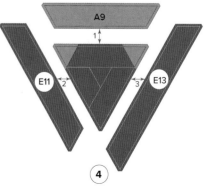

TOP EYES

Construct 2 eye units – Sew F1, D1, G2R, D4R, D4L, F4R and F4L together in the order indicated **(5)**. Sew F7 to the top of each eye unit, then sew C6L to the left side of one eye unit and C6R to the right side of the other eye unit **(6–7)**.

BOTTOM EYES

Construct 2 eye units – Sew G3, D1, D4R, D4L, F4R, F4L and F7 together in the order indicated **(8)**.

Construct 2 belly units – Sew B1, B3 and B5 together **(9)**.

Finish the left-facing eye – Sew 1 eye unit, 1 belly unit, C5, C6R and C9 together in the order indicated **(10)**.

Finish the right-facing eye – Sew the remaining eye unit, belly unit, C5, C6L and C9 together in the order indicated **(11)**.

TOP BODY

Sew 2 pieces A8R together, sew B13 and B15 together and sew 2 pieces A8L together **(12)**. Sew the units just made together **(12)**.

BOTTOM BODY

Construct the left-facing wing unit – Sew 3 pieces G1, 2 pieces A1 and A4R together **(13)**; sew the unit just made and 3 pieces A9 together with right-alignment, pressing the seams to the shorter side **(15)**.

Construct the right-facing wing unit — Sew 3 pieces G1, 2 pieces A1 and A4L together **(14)**; sew the unit just made and 3 pieces A9 together with left-alignment, pressing the seams to the shorter side **(15)**.

Construct the belly unit — Sew B9, B11, B13 and B15 together **(15)**. Sew the belly and wing units together **(15)**.

FINAL ASSEMBLY AND QUILTING

Sew all the units together in the order indicated **(16)**, pressing the beak seams towards the center. Finish your rug without binding and quilt it as you like (see Useful Information: Rug Without Binding). Add a non-slip backing if desired (see Additional Ideas).

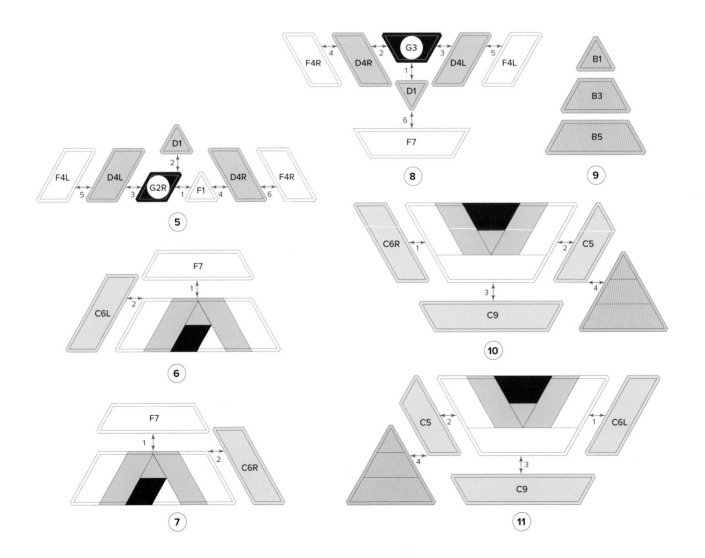

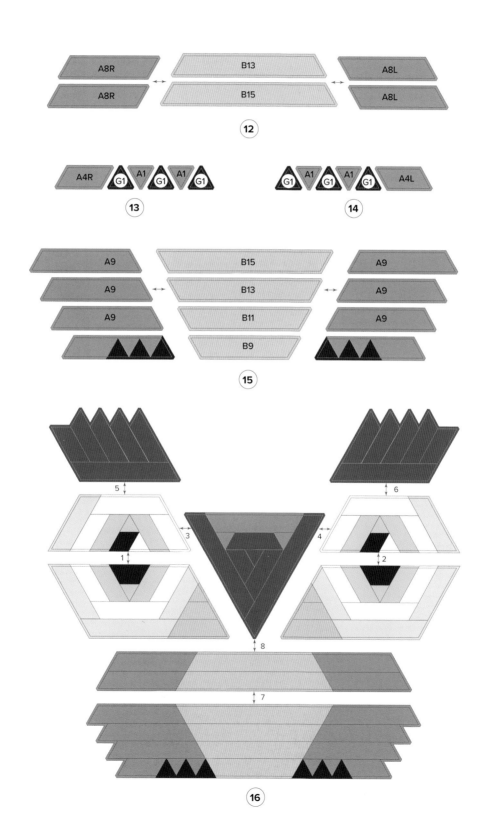

12

13   14

15

16

WALL HANGING

Materials

A: 4–5 dark purple strips (2½in x WOF) or ½yd

B: 4 light purple strips (2½in x WOF) or ½yd

C: 2 light blue strips (2½in x WOF) or ¼yd

D: 2 medium green strips (2½in x WOF) or ¼yd

E: 4 medium blue strips (2½in x WOF) or ½yd

F: 3 white strips (2½in x WOF) or ¼yd

G: 1 dark blue strip (2½in x WOF) or fabric scraps

H: 8 light neutral strips (2½in x WOF) or ¾yd

Backing: 1½yd

Binding: 5 strips (2½in x WOF) or ½yd

Finished Size

46 x 34in

CUTTING FABRICS

Cut the shapes from fabrics A–G as described for the Area Rug, then cut the background pieces from fabric H as follows.

H Use 8 light neutral strips (2½in x WOF)

H17 Cut 1 piece: 2½ x 21½in; trim to create an isosceles trapezoid.

H15 Cut 1 piece: 2½ x 19in; trim to create an isosceles trapezoid.

H13 Cut 1 piece: 2½ x 16¾in; trim to create an isosceles trapezoid.

H11 Cut 1 piece: 2½ x 14½in; trim to create an isosceles trapezoid.

HH6R & HH6L Cut 2 pieces: 2½ x 8¾in; trim to create 1 right-leaning trapezoid and 1 left-leaning trapezoid.

HH5R & HH5L Cut 6 pieces: 2½ x 7½in; trim to create 3 right-leaning trapezoids and 3 left-leaning trapezoids.

HH4R & HH4L Cut 10 pieces: 2½ x 6½in; trim to create 5 right-leaning trapezoids and 5 left-leaning trapezoids.

HH3R & HH3L Cut 10 pieces: 2½ x 5¼in; trim to create 5 right-leaning trapezoids and 5 left-leaning trapezoids.

HH2R & HH2L Cut 6 pieces: 2½ x 4in; trim to create 3 right-leaning trapezoids and 3 left-leaning trapezoids.

H1 Cut 8 equilateral triangles.

PIECING AND QUILTING

Sew with a ¼in seam allowance, pressing the seams open.

EYEBROWS
Construct the left-leaning eyebrow – Sew E5 on the right of H1 (1 eyebrow unit made); finish 3 more units in the same manner **(17)**. Sew HH2L and HH3L together, then sew E4R and HH3L in the order indicated to create the upper left corner **(19)**. Sew the upper left corner and 4 eyebrow units together (Row 1); sew HH4L and E10L together (Row 2); sew these 2 rows together **(21)**.

Construct the right-leaning eyebrow – Sew E5 on the left of H1 (1 eyebrow unit made); finish 3 more units in the same manner **(18)**. Sew HH2R and HH3R together, then sew E4L and HH3R in the order indicated to create the upper right corner **(20)**. Sew the upper right corner and 4 eyebrow units together (Row 1); sew HH4R and E10R together (Row 2); sew these 2 rows together **(22)**.

BEAK, TOP EYES, BOTTOM EYES AND TOP BODY
Same as for the Area Rug **(3–12)**.

BOTTOM BODY

Construct the belly unit – Sew B9, B11, B13 and B15 together **(23)**.

Construct the left-facing wing unit – Sew HH3R and A9 together (Row 1); sew HH4R and A9 together (Row 2); sew HH5R and A9 together (Row 3); sew HH6R, A4R, 3 pieces G1 and 2 pieces A1 together (Row 4). Sew these 4 rows together **(24)**. When sewing rows, align the 60° / 120° corners and sew to the side with right angles.

Do not worry if the sides with the right angles do not match up perfectly as they will be trimmed later.

Construct the right-facing wing unit – Sew HH3L and A9 together (Row 1); sew HH4L and A9 together (Row 2); sew HH5L and A9 together (Row 3); sew HH6L, A4L, 3 pieces G1 and 2 pieces A1 together (Row 4). Sew these 4 rows together **(25)** in the same manner as for the left-facing wing unit.

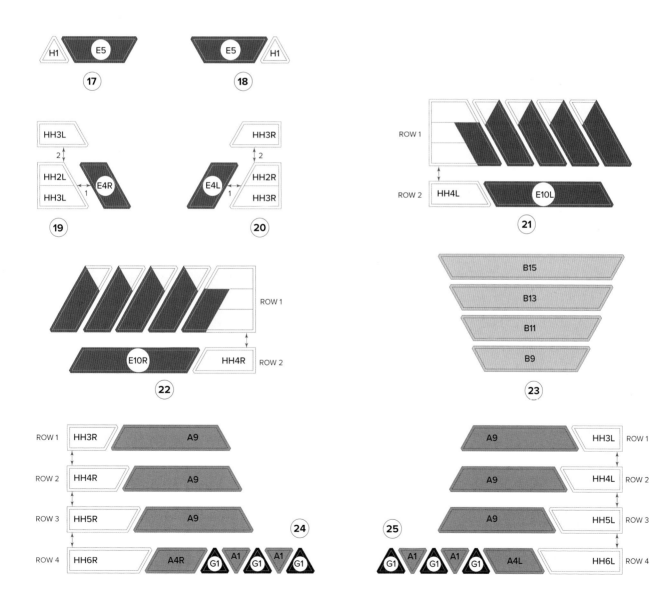

FINAL ASSEMBLY

In the following instructions, when piecing the right and left-leaning trapezoids, always align their 60° / 120° corners and sew to the side with the right angles.

Construct the background units – Sew H11, H13, H15 and H17 together; sew HH2R, HH3R and HH4R together; sew HH2L, HH3L and HH4L together; sew HH2R, HH3R, HH4R and HH5R together; sew HH2L, HH3L, HH4L and HH5L together; sew HH4R and HH5R together; sew HH4L and HH5L together **(26)**.

Sew all the units together in the order indicated **(26)**, aligning all intersecting points using pins and do not worry about matching up the side edges. Square up the finished top.

QUILTING AND BINDING

Make a quilt sandwich and quilt it as you like (see Useful Information). Bind your wall hanging using 5 strips 2½in x WOF (see Useful Information: Binding Rectangular Quilts). Add a few picture hanging strips to display the finished piece on the wall (see Additional Ideas: Wall Hanging).

The wall hanging could become a small rug for a reading corner in the playroom.

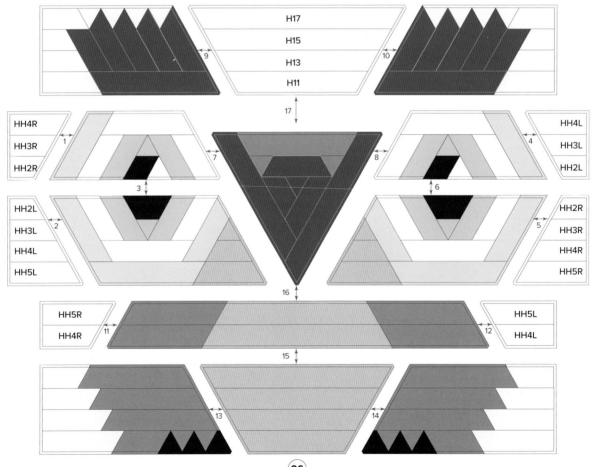

Quilt

Materials

A: 5 dark purple strips (2½in x WOF) or ½yd

B: 5 light purple strips (2½in x WOF) or ½yd

C: 3 light blue strips (2½in x WOF) or ¼yd

D: 3 medium green strips (2½in x WOF) or ¼yd

E: 5 medium blue strips (2½in x WOF) or ½yd

F: 3 white strips (2½in x WOF) or ¼yd

G: 1 dark blue strip (2½in x WOF) or fabric scraps

H: 12 light neutral strips (2½in x WOF) + 2yd or 3yd in total

Backing: 4½yd

Binding: 7 strips (2½in x WOF) or ¾yd

Finished Size

65 x 69in

CUTTING FABRICS

Make 1 owl block as described for the Wall Hanging, then cut the remaining fabrics as follows.

A, B, C, D Use 4 various strips (2½in x WOF)

A5, B5, C5, D5 Cut 8 pieces (2 from each strip): 2½ x 7½in; trim to create isosceles trapezoids.

A3, B3, C3, D3 Cut 8 pieces (2 from each strip): 2½ x 5¼in; trim to create isosceles trapezoids.

A1, B1, C1, D1 Cut 8 equilateral triangles (2 from each strip).

E Use 1 medium blue strip (2½in x WOF)

E-6in Cut 6 pieces: 2½ x 6in.

H Use 4 light neutral strips (2½in x WOF)

H5 Cut 9 pieces: 2½ x 7½in; trim to create isosceles trapezoids.

H3 Cut 9 pieces: 2½ x 5¼in; trim to create isosceles trapezoids.

H1 Cut 9 equilateral triangles.

H Use additional light neutral fabric (2yd)

Cut the border pieces as follows:

Horizontal Quilt Border Cut 2 strips 10in x WOF. Cut away selvages and sew 2 strips together along the short sides, step 1 **(31)**.

Horizontal and Vertical Block Border Cut away selvages, then cut 4 strips 10in x LOF.

PIECING AND QUILTING

Sew with a ¼in seam allowance unless otherwise indicated, pressing the seams open.

BANNER BORDER

Construct 8 flag units – Sew A1–D1, A3–D3 and A5–D5 together in the desired color order **(27)**.

Construct 9 background units – Sew H1, H3 and H5 together **(28)**.

Construct 2 side units – Sew 3 pieces E-6in together **(29)**.

Construct border – Sew 8 flags and 9 background units together, then square up the left and right edges **(30)**. Sew the side units on each side of the banner border, steps 2 and 3 **(31)**.

FINAL ASSEMBLY

Referring to Useful Information: Borders, trim the edges of the horizontal block borders to the width of your owl block and sew them to the top and bottom edges, steps 4 and 5 **(31)**. Trim the edges of the vertical block borders to the height of the owl block with horizontal block borders attached and sew them on each side, steps 6 and 7 **(31)**.

Sew the joined horizontal quilt borders to the bottom of the banner border, aligning from the center out, step 8 **(31)**. Trim the edges of this new border unit to the width of your owl quilt with borders attached and sew it to the bottom edge, step 9 **(31)**.

QUILTING AND BINDING

Cut the backing fabric in half across WOF. Cut away selvages and sew 2 pieces together along the long sides with a ½in seam allowance; press the seam open. Make a quilt sandwich and quilt it as you like (see Useful Information). Bind your quilt using 7 strips 2½in x WOF (see Useful Information: Binding Rectangular Quilts).

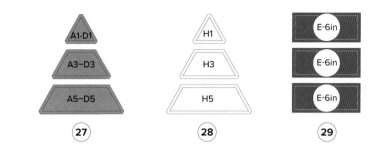

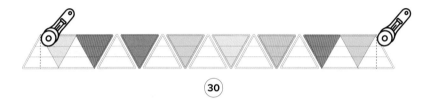

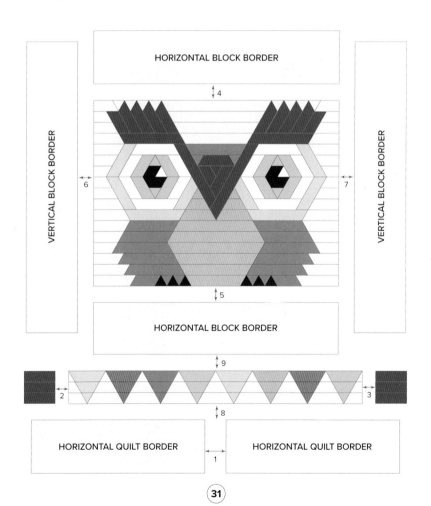

EXTRAS

BANNER

Make a colorful banner from your fabric leftovers. Use flag units from the Quilt to construct 7–8 flags **(27)**. Each finished flag measures 6in vertically and 7in horizontally, so you can estimate the length for your banner. Finish the banner as described in Additional Ideas: Banner.

PLACEMAT

Using 6 partial strips in various colors A–D, construct 6 flag units as for the Quilt **(27)**. Sew 3 flag units together to make 2 half-hexagons, then sew the half-hexagons together. Make a quilt sandwich and quilt it as you like. Bind your placemat using 2 strips 2½in x WOF (see Useful Information: Binding 120° Corners).

LOYAL DOG

Cuddle up to your canine best friend on this loyal dog lap quilt. A cute area rug can become a special place for creating long-lasting memories, allowing your pup to rest or play with toys. The bone motif can be used to create a doggy bowl mat to provide kibble and water as well. Use your fabric scraps to sew a coordinating banner for your favourite room, or add a pillow to your bundle by improvising the bowl mat pattern.

This theme features Northcott Stonehenge Gradations Strip Pack (Onyx) and Shimmer Radiance Single Colorway. Piecing and quilting are done using Aurifil 50wt cotton thread in coordinating colors.

Color Key

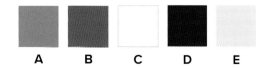

A   B   C   D   E

AREA RUG

Materials

A: 10 light brown strips (2½in x WOF) or ¾yd

B: 4 dark brown strips (2½in x WOF) or ½yd

C: 4 white strips (2½in x WOF) or ½yd

D: 1 black strip (2½in x WOF) or fabric scraps

Backing: 1½yd

Finished Size

43 x 38in

CUTTING FABRICS

A Use 10 light brown strips (2½in x WOF)

A14R & A14L Cut 2 pieces: 2½ x 18in; trim to create 1 right-leaning parallelogram and 1 left-leaning parallelogram.

A8R & A8L Cut 6 pieces: 2½ x 11in; trim to create 3 right-leaning parallelograms and 3 left-leaning parallelograms.

A7 Cut 3 pieces: 2½ x 9¾in; trim to create isosceles trapezoids.

A6R & A6L Cut 10 pieces: 2½ x 8¾in; trim to create 5 right-leaning parallelograms and 5 left-leaning parallelograms.

A5 Cut 9 pieces: 2½ x 7½in; trim to create isosceles trapezoids.

A4R & A4L Cut 2 pieces: 2½ x 6½in; trim to create 1 right-leaning parallelogram and 1 left-leaning parallelogram.

A3 Cut 7 pieces: 2½ x 5¼in; trim to create isosceles trapezoids.

A-3in Cut 2 pieces: 2½ x 3in.

A1 Cut 11 equilateral triangles.

B Use 4 dark brown strips (2½in x WOF)

B13 Cut 2 pieces: 2½ x 16¾in; trim to create isosceles trapezoids.

B11 Cut 2 pieces: 2½ x 14½in; trim to create isosceles trapezoids.

B9 Cut 2 pieces: 2½ x 12¼in; trim to create isosceles trapezoids.

B7 Cut 2 pieces: 2½ x 9¾in; trim to create isosceles trapezoids.

B5 Cut 2 pieces: 2½ x 7½in; trim to create isosceles trapezoids.

B3 Cut 2 pieces: 2½ x 5¼in; trim to create isosceles trapezoids.

C Use 4 white strips (2½in x WOF)

C13 Cut 1 piece: 2½ x 16¾in; trim to create an isosceles trapezoid.

C7 Cut 1 piece: 2½ x 9¾in; trim to create an isosceles trapezoid.

CC7R & CC7L Cut 2 pieces: 2½ x 9¾in; trim to create 1 right-leaning trapezoid and 1 left-leaning trapezoid.

C6R & C6L Cut 7 pieces: 2½ x 8¾in; trim to create 3 right-leaning parallelograms and 4 left-leaning parallelograms.

C5 Cut 2 pieces: 2½ x 7½in; trim to create isosceles trapezoids.

C3 Cut 1 piece: 2½ x 5¼in; trim to create an isosceles trapezoid.

C1 Cut 3 equilateral triangles.

D Use 1 black strip (2½in x WOF)

D5 Cut 1 piece: 2½ x 7½in; trim to create an isosceles trapezoid.

D3 Cut 3 pieces: 2½ x 5¼in; trim to create isosceles trapezoids.

D2L Cut 1 piece: 2½ x 4in; trim to create a left-leaning parallelogram.

D1 Cut 3 equilateral triangles.

PIECING AND QUILTING

Sew with a ¼in seam allowance, pressing the seams open unless otherwise indicated.

EARS
Construct 2 ear units – Sew A1, B3, B5, B7, B9, B11 and B13 together **(1)**.

FOREHEAD
Construct 5 triangle units – Sew A1, A3 and A5 together **(2)**.

Construct 1 left-leaning unit – Sew 2 of the triangle units just made and 5 pieces A6L together **(3)**.

Construct 1 right-leaning unit – Sew 2 of the triangle units just made and 5 pieces A6R together **(4)**. You should have 1 triangle unit left (center unit).

TOP OF FACE
Construct 1 left-facing eye – Sew A4R, 2 pieces D1, C1 and A1 together (Row 1); sew A5 and D3 together (Row 2); sew these 2 rows together **(5)**.

Construct 1 right-facing eye – Sew A1, D3 and A4L together (Row 1); sew D2L, C1 and A5 together; sew these 2 rows together **(6)**.

Construct 1 patch unit – Sew C1, C3, C5 and C7 together **(7)**.

Construct 2 head units – Sew A1, A3, A5 and A7 together **(8)**.

If you like having fun with colors, use slightly different shades of brown or various fabric prints, referring to the final layout to plan your cutting.

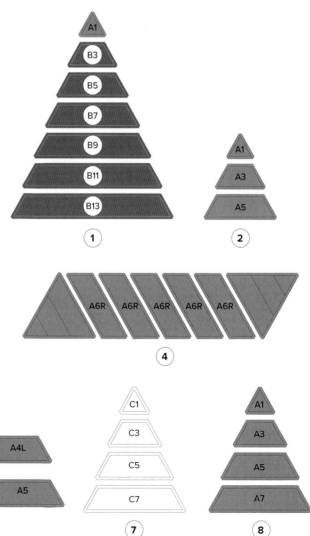

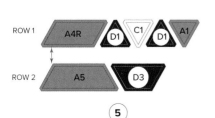

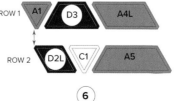

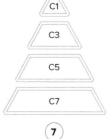

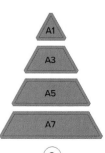

BOTTOM OF FACE

Construct the top of the muzzle
– Sew 2 pieces A-3in, CC7R,
D5 and CC7L together **(9)**.

Construct the bottom of the muzzle
– Sew D1, D3, C5, 3 pieces C6R,
4 pieces C6L, C13, A8R and A8L
together in the order indicated **(10)**.

FINAL ASSEMBLY AND QUILTING

Sew A14R, A14L, A7, 2 pieces A8R, 2 pieces A8L and all the
units you made together in the order indicated **(11)**. Press
the seams in steps 3 and 4 to the center piece. Using a ruler
with curved edges or a small round plate, round up the points
around the muzzle **(11)**. Finish your rug without binding and
quilt it as you like (see Useful Information: Rug Without Binding).
Add a non-slip backing if desired (see Additional Ideas).

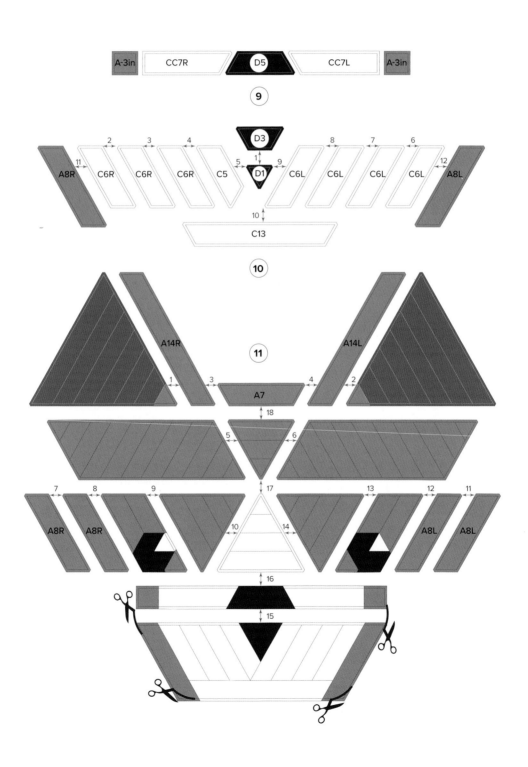

WALL HANGING

Materials

A: 10 light brown strips (2½in x WOF) or ¾yd

B: 4 dark brown strips (2½in x WOF) or ½yd

C: 4 white strips (2½in x WOF) or ½yd

D: 1 black strip (2½in x WOF) or fabric scraps

E: 12 light blue strips (2½in x WOF) or 1yd

Backing: 1½yd

Binding: 5 strips (2½in x WOF) or ½yd

Finished Size

47 x 38in

CUTTING FABRICS

Cut the shapes from fabrics A–D as described for the Area Rug, then cut the background pieces from fabric E as follows.

E Use 12 light blue strips (2½in x WOF)

E19 Cut 1 piece: 2½ x 23¾in; trim to create an isosceles trapezoid.

E17 Cut 1 piece: 2½ x 21½in; trim to create an isosceles trapezoid.

E15 Cut 1 piece: 2½ x 19in; trim to create an isosceles trapezoid.

E13 Cut 1 piece: 2½ x 16¾in; trim to create an isosceles trapezoid.

EE12R & EE12L Cut 2 pieces: 2½ x 15½in; trim to create 1 right-leaning trapezoid and 1 left-leaning trapezoid.

E11 Cut 1 piece: 2½ x 14½in; trim to create an isosceles trapezoid.

EE11R & EE11L Cut 2 pieces: 2½ x 14½in; trim to create 1 right-leaning trapezoid and 1 left-leaning trapezoid.

EE10R & EE10L Cut 2 pieces: 2½ x 13¼in; trim to create 1 right-leaning trapezoid and 1 left-leaning trapezoid.

E9 Cut 1 piece: 2½ x 12¼in; trim to create an isosceles trapezoid.

EE9R & EE9L Cut 2 pieces: 2½ x 12¼in; trim to create 1 right-leaning trapezoid and 1 left-leaning trapezoid.

E-11in Cut 2 pieces: 2½ x 11in.

EE8R & EE8L Cut 4 pieces: 2½ x 11in; trim to create 2 right-leaning trapezoids and 2 left-leaning trapezoids.

EE7R & EE7L Cut 4 pieces: 2½ x 9¾in; trim to create 2 right-leaning trapezoids and 2 left-leaning trapezoids.

EE6R & EE6L Cut 4 pieces: 2½ x 8¾in; trim to create 2 right-leaning trapezoids and 2 left-leaning trapezoids.

EE5R & EE5L Cut 4 pieces: 2½ x 7½in; trim to create 2 right-leaning trapezoids and 2 left-leaning trapezoids.

EE4R & EE4L Cut 4 pieces: 2½ x 6½in; trim to create 2 right-leaning trapezoids and 2 left-leaning trapezoids.

EE3R & EE3L Cut 4 pieces: 2½ x 5¼in; trim to create 2 right-leaning trapezoids and 2 left-leaning trapezoids.

EE2R & EE2L Cut 4 pieces: 2½ x 4in; trim to create 2 right-leaning trapezoids and 2 left-leaning trapezoids.

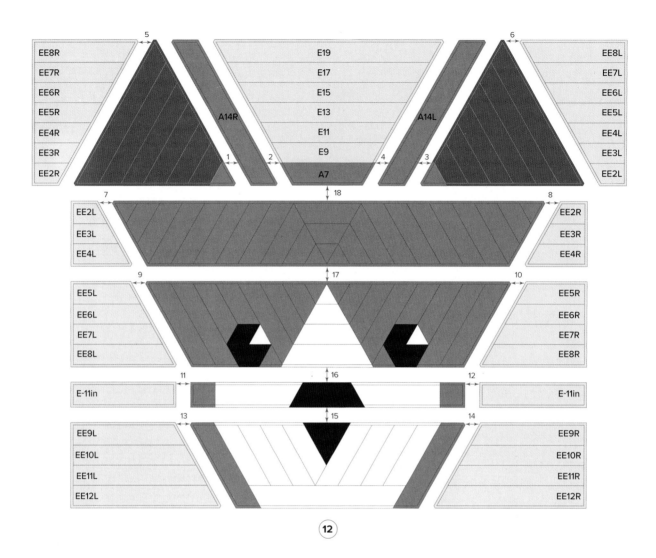

PIECING AND QUILTING

Sew with a ¼in seam allowance, pressing the seams open.

EARS, FOREHEAD, TOP AND BOTTOM OF FACE
Same as for the Area Rug **(1–10)**.

FINAL ASSEMBLY
Referring to Area Rug diagram **(11)**, continue as follows.

Assemble the forehead – Sew the center unit, right-leaning unit and left-leaning unit together (steps 5 and 6). Assemble the top of the face – Sew 2 pieces A8R, 2 pieces A8L, 2 eye units, 2 head units and the patch unit together (steps 7–14).

In the following instructions, when piecing the right and left-leaning trapezoids, always align their 60° / 120° corners and sew to the side with the right angles.

Construct the background units – Sew A7, E9, E11, E13, E15, E17 and E19 together; sew EE2R, EE3R, EE4R, EE5R, EE6R, EE7R and EE8R together; sew EE2L, EE3L, EE4L, EE5L, EE6L, EE7L and EE8L together;

sew EE2L, EE3L and EE4L together; sew EE2R, EE3R and EE4R together; sew EE5L, EE6L, EE7L and EE8L together; sew EE5R, EE6R, EE7R and EE8R together; sew EE9L, EE10L, EE11L and EE12L together; sew EE9R, EE10R, EE11R and EE12R together **(12)**.

Sew A14R, A14L, 2 pieces E-11in and all the finished units together in the order indicated **(12)**. When sewing rows (steps 15–18), align all intersecting points using pins and do not worry about matching up the side edges. Square up the finished top.

QUILTING AND BINDING
Make a quilt sandwich and quilt it as you like (see Useful Information). Bind your wall hanging using 5 strips 2½in x WOF (see Useful Information: Binding Rectangular Quilts). Add a few picture hanging strips to display the finished piece on the wall (see Additional Ideas: Wall Hanging).

BOWL MAT

Materials

C: 2 white strips (2½in x WOF) or ¼yd

E: 3 light blue strips (2½in x WOF) or ½yd

Backing: 24 x 15in

Binding: 2 strips (2½in x WOF) or ¼yd

Finished Size

22 x 13in

CUTTING FABRICS

C Use 2 white strips (2½in x WOF)

C7 Cut 2 pieces: 2½ x 9¾in; trim to create isosceles trapezoids.

C-5in Cut 3 pieces: 2½ x 5in.

C5 Cut 2 pieces: 2½ x 7½in; trim to create isosceles trapezoids.

C3 Cut 4 pieces: 2½ x 5¼in; trim to create isosceles trapezoids.

E Use 3 light blue strips (2½in x WOF)

E-13½in Cut 2 pieces: 2½ x 13½in.

E-5in Cut 6 pieces: 2½ x 5in.

EE3R & EE3L Cut 4 pieces: 2½ x 5¼in; trim to create 2 right-leaning trapezoids and 2 left-leaning trapezoids.

EE2R & EE2L Cut 8 pieces: 2½ x 4in; trim to create 4 right-leaning trapezoids and 4 left-leaning trapezoids.

E1 Cut 2 equilateral triangles.

PIECING AND QUILTING

Sew with a ¼in seam allowance, pressing the seams open.

BONE BLOCK
Construct Rows 1 and 5 – Sew EE2R, 2 pieces C3, E1 and EE2L together **(13)**.

Construct Rows 2 and 4 – Sew EE2L and EE3L together; sew C5 and C7 together; sew EE2R and EE3R together; sew these 3 units together **(13)**.

Construct Row 3 – Sew 3 pieces E-5in together twice; sew 3 pieces C-5in together; sew these 3 units together **(13)**. Sew the 5 rows of the bone block together **(13)**. When sewing rows, align all the intersecting points using pins and do not worry about matching up the side edges. Square up your finished block to 18½ x 13½in.

FINAL ASSEMBLY, QUILTING AND BINDING
Holding the bone block horizontally, sew E-13½in to the left and right edges of the block. Make a quilt sandwich and quilt it as you like (see Useful Information). Bind the bowl mat using 2 strips 2½in x WOF (see Useful Information: Binding Rectangular Quilts).

ROW 1 | EE2R | C3 | E1 | C3 | EE2L

ROW 2 | EE2L | C7 | EE2R
EE3L | C5 | EE3R

ROW 3 | E-5in | C-5in | E-5in
E-5in | C-5in | E-5in
E-5in | C-5in | E-5in

ROW 4 | EE3R | C5 | EE3L
EE2R | C7 | EE2L

ROW 5 | EE2L | C3 | E1 | C3 | EE2R

13

Quilt

Materials

A: 10 light brown strips (2½in x WOF) or ¾yd

B: 4 dark brown strips (2½in x WOF) or ½yd

C: 4 white strips (2½in x WOF) or ½yd

D: 1 black strip (2½in x WOF) or fabric scraps

E: 17 light blue strips (2½in x WOF) + 1¼yd or 2¾yd in total

Backing: 4yd

Binding: 7 strips (2½ x WOF) or ¾yd

Finished Size

56 x 64in

CUTTING FABRICS

Make 1 dog block as described for the Wall Hanging. Make 2 bone blocks as described for the Bowl Mat, omitting the E-13½in borders. Then cut the additional fabric E pieces as follows.

E Use additional light blue fabric (1¼yd)

Cut away selvages, then cut the following border pieces:

Long Vertical Borders Cut 2 strips 4½in x WOF.

Horizontal and Short Vertical Borders Cut 2 strips 13½in x WOF. From each strip, cut 1 short vertical border 13½ x 4½in and mark the remaining part as horizontal border.

PIECING AND QUILTING

Sew with a ¼in seam allowance unless otherwise indicated, pressing the seams open.

FINAL ASSEMBLY

Referring to Useful Information: Borders, trim the edges of the long vertical borders to the height of your dog block and sew them on at each side, steps 1 and 2 **(14)**.

Construct 2 bone borders – Holding the bone block horizontally, sew the short vertical border to one side of the bone block and the horizontal border to the other side, steps 3–6 **(14)**. Trim the long edge of each bone border to the width of your quilt top and sew them to the top and bottom edges, steps 7 and 8 **(14)**.

QUILTING AND BINDING

Cut the backing fabric in half across WOF. Cut away selvages and sew 2 pieces together along the long sides with a ½in seam allowance; press the seam open. Make a quilt sandwich and quilt it as you like (see Useful Information). Bind your quilt using 7 strips 2½in x WOF (see Useful Information: Binding Rectangular Quilts).

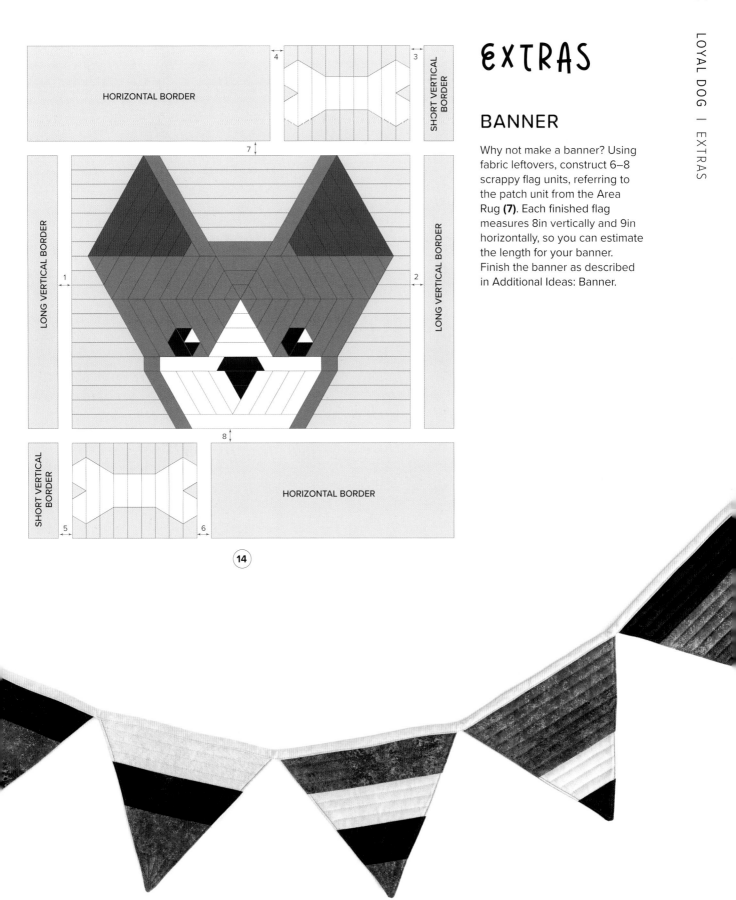

EXTRAS

BANNER

Why not make a banner? Using fabric leftovers, construct 6–8 scrappy flag units, referring to the patch unit from the Area Rug **(7)**. Each finished flag measures 8in vertically and 9in horizontally, so you can estimate the length for your banner. Finish the banner as described in Additional Ideas: Banner.

SASSY CAT

When you're feeling a little sassy, all you need is a feline friend and a cozy quilt, because anything is possible with a cat best friend. Make a little fish placemat for your snacks and enjoy snuggle time even more. For a complete set, finish an area rug for your room and dress up the wall with a colorful banner or a wall hanging. A soft bed pillow is also easy to make using fabrics leftover from your quilt.

This theme features Mixmasters Mashup Pinwheel by Patrick Lose, Mixmasters Mashup Single Colorway and Northcott Chroma Single Colorway. Piecing and quilting are done using Aurifil 50wt cotton thread in coordinating colors.

Color key

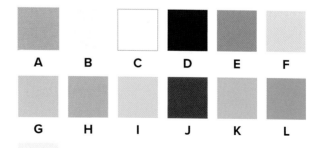

A   B   C   D   E   F

G   H   I   J   K   L

M

AREA RUG

Materials

A: 9 medium gray strips (2½in x WOF) or ¾yd

B: 3 light gray strips (2½in x WOF) or ¼yd

C: 1 white strip (2½in x WOF) or fabric scraps

D: 1 black strip (2½in x WOF) or fabric scraps

E, F, G, H: 4 colorful strips, 1 of each desired color (2½in x WOF) or fabric scraps

Backing: 1yd

Binding: ½yd of fabric or 135in of 2½in bias binding strip

Finished Size

32 x 32in

CUTTING FABRICS

A Use 9 medium gray strips (2½in x WOF)

A-33in Cut 3 pieces: 2½ x 33in.

A13 Cut 1 piece: 2½ x 16¾in; trim to create an isosceles trapezoid.

A11 Cut 3 pieces: 2½ x 14½in; trim to create isosceles trapezoids.

A9 Cut 3 pieces: 2½ x 12¼in; trim to create isosceles trapezoids.

A8R & A8L Cut 4 pieces: 2½ x 11in; trim to create 2 right-leaning parallelograms and 2 left-leaning parallelograms.

A6R & A6L Cut 2 pieces: 2½ x 8¾in; trim to create 1 right-leaning parallelogram and 1 left-leaning parallelogram.

AA6R & AA6L Cut 2 pieces: 2½ x 8¾in; trim to create 1 right-leaning trapezoid and 1 left-leaning trapezoid.

A5 Cut 1 piece: 2½ x 7½in; trim to create an isosceles trapezoid.

AA5R & AA5L Cut 2 pieces: 2½ x 7½in; trim to create 1 right-leaning trapezoid and 1 left-leaning trapezoid.

A-7½in Cut 2 pieces: 2½ x 7½in and trim each piece to 1½ x 7½in.

AA4R & AA4L Cut 2 pieces: 2½ x 6½in; trim to create 1 right-leaning trapezoid and 1 left-leaning trapezoid.

B Use 3 light gray strips (2½in x WOF)

B6R & B6L Cut 7 pieces: 2½ x 8¾in; trim to create 3 right-leaning parallelograms and 4 left-leaning parallelograms.

B5 Cut 1 piece: 2½ x 7½in; trim to create an isosceles trapezoid.

B-5¼in Cut 1 piece: 2½ x 5¼in and trim it to 1½ x 5¼in.

BB1R & BB1L Cut 2 pieces: 2½ x 3in; trim to create 1 right-leaning trapezoid and 1 left-leaning trapezoid.

B1 Cut 1 equilateral triangle.

C Use 1 white strip (2½in x WOF)

C1 Cut 2 equilateral triangles.

D Use 1 black strip (2½in x WOF)

D-7½in Cut 2 pieces: 2½ x 7½in and trim each piece to 1½ x 7½in.

D-5¼in Cut 1 piece: 2½ x 5¼in and trim it to 1½ x 5¼in.

D2R Cut 2 pieces: 2½ x 4in; trim to create 2 right-leaning parallelograms.

D1 Cut 1 equilateral triangle.

E, F, G, H Use 4 colorful strips, 1 of each desired color (2½in x WOF)

H7 Cut 2 pieces: 2½ x 9¾in; trim to create isosceles trapezoids.

G5 Cut 2 pieces: 2½ x 7½in; trim to create isosceles trapezoids.

F3 Cut 2 pieces: 2½ x 5¼in; trim to create isosceles trapezoids.

E1 Cut 2 equilateral triangles.

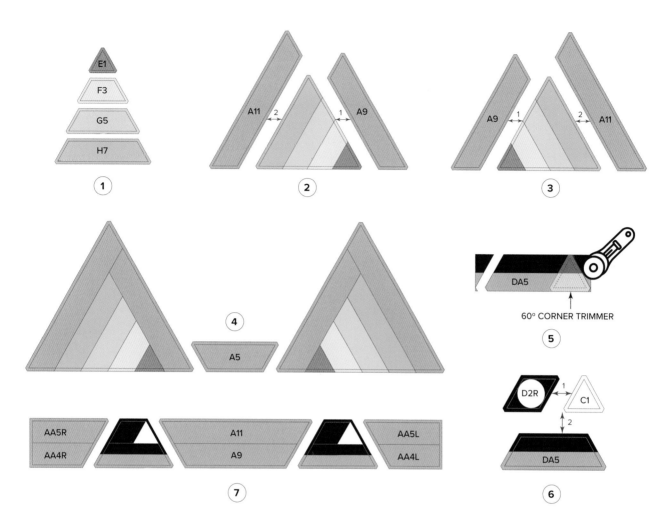

PIECING AND QUILTING

Sew with a ¼in seam allowance, pressing the seams open unless otherwise indicated.

HEAD CROWN AND EARS

Construct 2 ear units – Sew E1, F3, G5 and H7 together **(1)**. Finish the left-facing ear – Sew A9 and A11 to the first ear unit in the order indicated **(2)**. Finish the right-facing ear – Sew A9 and A11 to the second ear unit in the order indicated **(3)**. Sew the left-facing ear, right-facing ear and A5 together, pressing the seams to the center piece **(4)**.

EYES

Construct 2 DA5 units – Sew D-7½in and A-7½in together along the longest sides. With the black edge facing up, trim off the corners to create isosceles trapezoids **(5)**.

Construct 2 eyes – Sew D2R, C1 and DA5 together in the order indicated **(6)**. Finish the eyes unit – Sew AA4R and AA5R together; sew AA4L and AA5L together; sew A9 and A11 together; sew the units just made and the 2 eye units together **(7)**.

TOP MUZZLE

Construct 1 BD3 unit – Sew B-5¼in
and D-5¼in together along the longest
sides. With the black edge facing
down, trim off the corners to create
an isosceles trapezoid **(8)**. Sew AA6R,
B6R, BD3, B6L and AA6L together **(9)**.

FACE

Sew the top muzzle unit, eyes unit
and 3 strips A-33in together **(10)**.

CHIN

Construct the nose unit – Sew BB1R, D1
and BB1L together **(11)**; trim off the corners
to create an isosceles trapezoid **(12)**.

Construct the muzzle unit – Sew the
nose unit, B1, B5, 2 pieces B6R, 3
pieces B6L, A6R and A6L together in
the order indicated **(13)**. Sew A13, 2
pieces A8R and 2 pieces A8L to the
muzzle unit in the order indicated **(14)**.

If you prefer to finish
your rug without
binding, refer to
Useful Information:
Rug Without Binding.

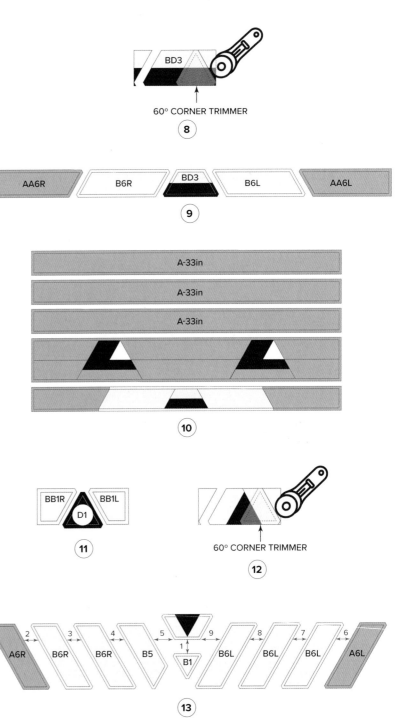

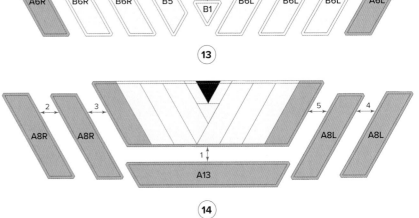

FINAL ASSEMBLY

Sew all the units together in
the order indicated (15).

QUILTING AND BINDING

Make a quilt sandwich and quilt it as you
like (see Useful Information). Trim away
the excess batting and backing around the
edges. Using a ruler with curved edges or
a round plate, round up the points around
the head, except the ears (15). Prepare a
bias binding, 135in in length (see Useful
Information: Bias Binding). Bind your rug
(see Useful Information: Binding Quilts
With Curved Edges). Add a non-slip
backing if desired (see Additional Ideas).

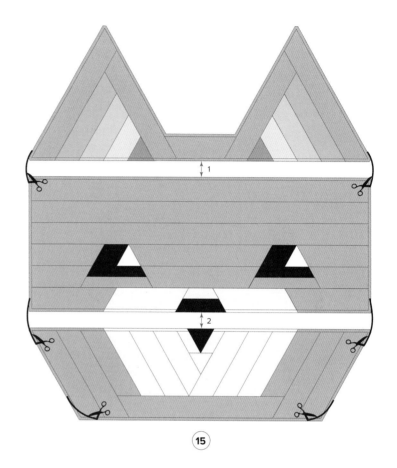

(15)

WALL HANGING

Materials

A: 9 medium gray strips (2½in x WOF) or ¾yd

B: 3 light gray strips (2½in x WOF) or ¼yd

C: 1 white strip (2½in x WOF) or fabric scraps

D: 1 black strip (2½in x WOF) or fabric scraps

E, F, G, H: 4 colorful strips, 1 of each desired color (2½in x WOF) or fabric scraps

I: 1 bright yellow strip (2½in x WOF) or fabric scraps

J: 1 bright red strip (2½in x WOF) or fabric scraps

M: 11 light neutral strips (2½in x WOF) or 1yd

Backing: 1¼yd

Binding: 5 strips (2½in x WOF) or ½yd

Finished Size

41 x 37in

CUTTING FABRICS

Cut the shapes from fabrics A–H as described for the Area Rug, then cut the additional pieces as follows.

I Use 1 bright yellow strip (2½in x WOF)

I3 Cut 2 pieces: 2½ x 5¼in; trim to create isosceles trapezoids.

J Use 1 bright red strip (2½in x WOF)

JJ8R & JJ8L Cut 2 pieces: 2½ x 11in; trim to create 1 right-leaning trapezoid and 1 left-leaning trapezoid.

M Use 11 light neutral strips (2½in x WOF)

MM16R & MM16L Cut 2 pieces: 2½ x 20¼in; trim to create 1 right-leaning trapezoid and 1 left-leaning trapezoid.

M15 Cut 1 piece: 2½ x 19in; trim to create an isosceles trapezoid.

M13 Cut 1 piece: 2½ x 16¾in; trim to create an isosceles trapezoid.

M11 Cut 1 piece: 2½ x 14½in; trim to create an isosceles trapezoid.

M9 Cut 1 piece: 2½ x 12¼in; trim to create an isosceles trapezoid.

MM9R & MM9L Cut 2 pieces: 2½ x 12¼in; trim to create 1 right-leaning trapezoid and 1 left-leaning trapezoid.

MM8R & MM8L Cut 2 pieces: 2½ x 11in; trim to create 1 right-leaning trapezoid and 1 left-leaning trapezoid.

M-9¾in Cut 2 pieces: 2½ x 9¾in.

M7 Cut 1 piece: 2½ x 9¾in; trim to create an isosceles trapezoid.

MM7R & MM7L Cut 4 pieces: 2½ x 9¾in; trim to create 2 right-leaning trapezoids and 2 left-leaning trapezoids.

MM6R & MM6L Cut 4 pieces: 2½ x 8¾in; trim to create 2 right-leaning trapezoids and 2 left-leaning trapezoids.

MM5R & MM5L Cut 4 pieces: 2½ x 7½in; trim to create 2 right-leaning trapezoids and 2 left-leaning trapezoids.

MM4R & MM4L Cut 4 pieces: 2½ x 6½in; trim to create 2 right-leaning trapezoids and 2 left-leaning trapezoids.

M-5¼in Cut 12 pieces: 2½ x 5¼in.

PIECING AND QUILTING

Sew with a ¼in seam allowance, pressing the seams open.

EARS, FACE AND CHIN

Construct 2 ear units as for the Area Rug **(1–3)**, but do not sew them together yet. Finish the face and chin as for the Area Rug **(5–14)**.

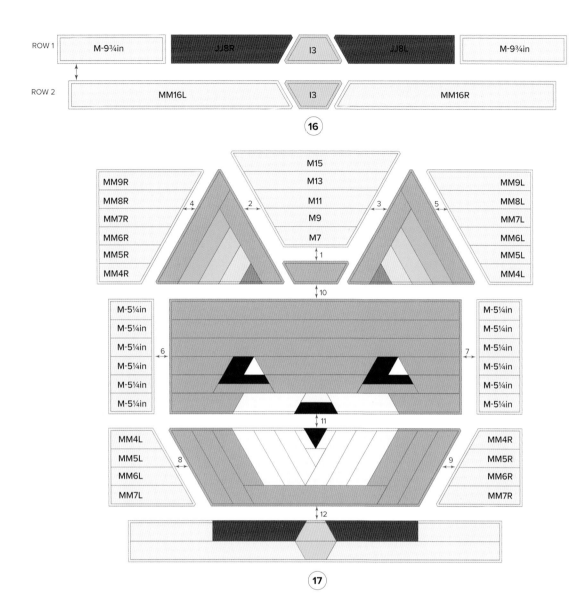

COLLAR

Sew JJ8R, I3, JJ8L, and 2 pieces M-9¾in together
(Row 1); sew MM16L, I3 and MM16R together
(Row 2); sew Row 1 and Row 2 together **(16)**.

FINAL ASSEMBLY

In the following instructions, when piecing the right
and left-leaning trapezoids, always align their 60° / 120°
corners and sew to the side with the right angles.

Construct the background units – Sew M7, M9, M11,
M13 and M15 together; sew MM4R, MM5R, MM6R,
MM7R, MM8R and MM9R together; sew MM4L,
MM5L, MM6L, MM7L, MM8L and MM9L together;
sew MM4L, MM5L, MM6L and MM7L together;
sew MM4R, MM5R, MM6R and MM7R together;
sew 6 pieces M-5¼in together twice **(17)**.

Sew all the units together in the order indicated **(17)**.
When sewing rows (steps 10–12), align all intersecting
points using pins and do not worry about matching
up the side edges. Square up the finished top.

QUILTING AND BINDING

Make a quilt sandwich and quilt it as you like (see Useful
Information). Bind your wall hanging using 5 strips 2½in x
WOF (see Useful Information: Binding Rectangular Quilts).
Add a few picture hanging strips to display the finished
piece on the wall (see Additional Ideas: Wall Hanging).

QuilT

Materials

A: 18 medium gray strips (2½in x WOF) or 1½yd

B: 5 light gray strips (2½in x WOF) or ½yd

C: 1 white strip (2½in x WOF) or fabric scraps

D: 2 black strips (2½in x WOF) or ¼yd

E, F, G, H: 4 colorful strips, 1 of each desired color (2½in x WOF) or fabric scraps

I: 1 bright yellow strip (2½in x WOF) or fabric scraps

J: 2 bright red strips (2½in x WOF) or ¼yd

K, L: 4 light (K) and 4 dark (L) strips in various colors (2½in x WOF) or fabric scraps

M: 28 light neutral strips (2½in x WOF) + 2yd or 4yd in total

Backing: 5yd

Binding: 8 strips (2½in x WOF) or ¾yd

Finished Size

65 x 87in

CUTTING FABRICS

Make 2 cat blocks as described for the Wall Hanging, then cut the additional pieces as follows.

K Use 4 light strips in various colors (2½in x WOF)

K2R & K2L From each strip, cut 2 pieces: 2½ x 4in; trim to create 1 right-leaning parallelogram and 1 left-leaning parallelogram.
K3 From each strip, cut 2 pieces: 2½ x 5¼in; trim to create isosceles trapezoids.

L Use 4 dark strips in various colors (2½in x WOF)

L2R & L2L From each strip, cut 2 pieces: 2½ x 4in; trim to create 1 right-leaning parallelogram and 1 left-leaning parallelogram.

M Use 6 light neutral strips (2½in x WOF)

M-15in Cut 8 pieces: 2½ x 15in.
MM2R & MM2L Cut 16 pieces: 2½ x 4in; trim to create 8 right-leaning trapezoids and 8 left-leaning trapezoids.
M1 Cut 8 equilateral triangles.

M Use additional light neutral fabric (2yd)

Cut away selvages, then cut the following background pieces:
Cat Block Borders Cut 3 strips 5in x WOF.
Big Blocks Cut 1 strip 25in x LOF and sub-cut into 2 squares 25 x 25in.
Small Blocks Cut 1 strip 8½in x LOF and sub-cut into 4 rectangles 8½ x 10½in.
Fish Block Border Cut 1 strip 5in x LOF and trim it to 5 x 25in.

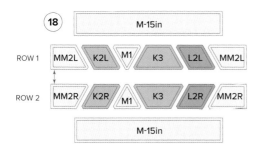

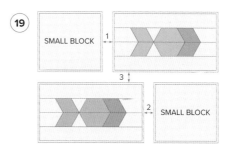

PIECING AND QUILTING

Sew with a ¼in seam allowance unless otherwise indicated, pressing the seams open.

FISH BLOCKS

Construct 4 blocks, using the light colorful pieces K for the fish bodies and the dark colorful pieces L for the fish heads – Sew MM2L, K2L, M1, K3, L2L and MM2L together (Row 1); sew MM2R, K2R, M1, K3, L2R and MM2R together (Row 2); sew these 2 rows together and square up the block to 4½ x 15in; sew M-15in to the top and bottom edges **(18)**.

FINAL ASSEMBLY, QUILTING AND BINDING

Construct 2 fish units – Sew 2 fish blocks and 2 small blocks together in the order indicated **(19)**. Trim the edges of the 3 cat block borders to the width of your cat blocks. Sew all the pieces together in the order indicated **(20)**. Cut the backing fabric in half across WOF. Cut away selvages and sew 2 pieces together along the long sides with a ½in seam allowance; press the seam open. Make a quilt sandwich and quilt it as you like (see Useful Information). Bind your quilt using 8 strips 2½in x WOF (see Useful Information: Binding Rectangular Quilts).

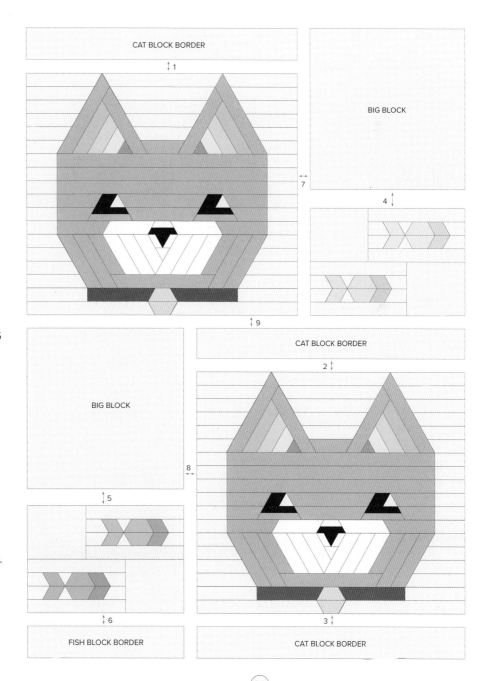

PLACEMAT

Materials

K, L: 1 light (K) and 1 dark (L) strip (2½in x WOF) or fabric scraps

M: 3 light neutral strips (2½in x WOF) or ¼yd

Backing: 17 x 14in

Binding: 2 strips (2½in x WOF) or ¼yd

Finished Size

15 x 12in

CUTTING FABRICS

K Use 1 light strip (2½in x WOF)

K2R & K2L Cut 2 pieces: 2½ x 4in; trim to create 1 right-leaning parallelogram and 1 left-leaning parallelogram.

K3 Cut 2 pieces: 2½ x 5¼in; trim to create isosceles trapezoids.

L Use 1 dark strip (2½in x WOF)

L2R & L2L Cut 2 pieces: 2½ x 4in; trim to create 1 right-leaning parallelogram and 1 left-leaning parallelogram.

M Use 3 light neutral strips (2½in x WOF)

M-15in Cut 4 pieces: 2½ x 15in.

MM2R & MM2L Cut 4 pieces: 2½ x 4in; trim to create 2 right-leaning trapezoids and 2 left-leaning trapezoids.

M1 Cut 2 equilateral triangles.

PIECING AND QUILTING

Sew with a ¼in seam allowance, pressing the seams open.

FINAL ASSEMBLY
Make 1 fish block as for the Quilt **(18)**, then sew M-15in to the top and bottom edges **(21)**.

QUITING AND BINDING
Make a quilt sandwich and quilt it as you like. Bind your placemat using 2 strips 2½in x WOF (see Useful Information: Binding Rectangular Quilts).

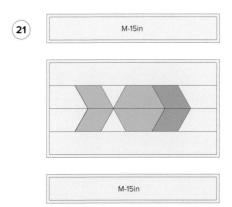

EXTRAS

PILLOWCASE

You will need colorful fabric scraps for fish, 8 strips for background plus fabrics for backing and binding. For a rectangular pillowcase, make 2 fish blocks from the Quilt and cut 12 additional pieces M-15in (2½ x 15in). Sew 2 pieces M-15in to the bottom edge and 4 pieces M-15in to the top edge of each fish block. Turn one of the blocks 180°, so that the fish are facing towards each other, and sew the blocks together **(22)**. Finish your pillowcase as described in Additional Ideas: Pillowcase.

BANNER

The banner is made from fabric leftovers, using colorful fabric strips E, F, G and H. Construct 6–7 flag units referring to the ear units from the cat block in the Area Rug **(1)**. Each finished flag measures 8in vertically and 9in horizontally, so you can estimate the length for your banner. Rotate every flag to create a random pattern layout in the banner. Finish the banner as described in Additional Ideas: Banner.

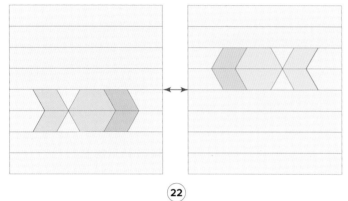

22

MISCHIEVOUS RACCOON

Never feel guilty about snacking and reading, because nothing can beat the happiness of enjoying a good book under the covers with tea and biscuits close to hand. The mischievous raccoon quilt will add extra personality to your happy place, so just cozy up and dive into reading. Why not make a matching reading rug for your little ones, to enhance the imaginative adventures of their bedtime stories? The contemporary placemat and a banner with black and white accents are wonderful beginner-friendly projects, too.

This theme features Northcott Stonehenge Gradations Strip Pack (Graphite) and Canvas Single Colorway. Piecing and quilting are done using Aurifil 50wt cotton thread in coordinating colors.

Color key

A   B   C   D   E

AREA RUG

Materials

A: 5 dark gray strips (2½in x WOF) or ½yd

B: 3 light gray strips (2½in x WOF) or ¼yd

C: 3 white strips (2½in x WOF) or ¼yd

D: 3 black strips (2½in x WOF) or ¼yd

Backing: 1yd

Finished Size

39 x 26in

CUTTING FABRICS

A Use 5 dark gray strips (2½in x WOF)

A19 Cut 1 piece: 2½ x 23¾in; trim to create an isosceles trapezoid.

A12R & A12L Cut 2 pieces: 2½ x 15½in; trim to create 1 right-leaning parallelogram and 1 left-leaning parallelogram.

A7 Cut 1 piece: 2½ x 9¾in; trim to create an isosceles trapezoid.

A6R & A6L Cut 2 pieces: 2½ x 8¾in; trim to create 1 right-leaning parallelogram and 1 left-leaning parallelogram.

A5 Cut 3 pieces: 2½ x 7½in; trim to create isosceles trapezoids.

A3 Cut 8 pieces: 2½ x 5¼in; trim to create isosceles trapezoids.

A1 Cut 6 equilateral triangles.

B Use 3 light gray strips (2½in x WOF)

B11 Cut 1 piece: 2½ x 14½in; trim to create an isosceles trapezoid.

B10R & B10L Cut 2 pieces: 2½ x 13¼in; trim to create 1 right-leaning parallelogram and 1 left-leaning parallelogram.

B9 Cut 2 pieces: 2½ x 12¼in; trim to create isosceles trapezoids.

B7 Cut 3 pieces: 2½ x 9¾in; trim to create isosceles trapezoids.

B3 Cut 2 pieces: 2½ x 5¼in; trim to create isosceles trapezoids.

B1 Cut 2 equilateral triangles.

C Use 3 white strips (2½in x WOF)

C7 Cut 5 pieces: 2½ x 9¾in; trim to create isosceles trapezoids.

C5 Cut 5 pieces: 2½ x 7½in; trim to create isosceles trapezoids.

C3 Cut 2 pieces: 2½ x 5¼in; trim to create isosceles trapezoids.

C1 Cut 3 equilateral triangles.

D Use 3 black strips (2½in x WOF)

D7 Cut 2 pieces: 2½ x 9¾in; trim to create isosceles trapezoids.

D5 Cut 4 pieces: 2½ x 7½in; trim to create isosceles trapezoids.

D3 Cut 3 pieces: 2½ x 5¼in; trim to create isosceles trapezoids.

DD3R & DD3L Cut 4 pieces: 2½ x 5¼in; trim to create 2 right-leaning trapezoids and 2 left-leaning trapezoids.

D1 Cut 4 equilateral triangles.

PIECING AND QUILTING

Sew with a ¼in seam allowance, pressing the seams open unless otherwise indicated.

EARS AND HEAD CROWN

Construct 2 ear units – Sew D1, D3, D5, D7 and B9 together **(1)**. Finish the head crown – Sew 2 ear units, B10R, B10L and A7 together in the order indicated **(2)**, pressing the seams to the center piece in steps 3 and 4.

EYES

Construct 2 eye units – Sew DD3R, C1 and DD3L together **(3)**; from the finished unit, trim off the corners to create an isosceles trapezoid **(4)**; sew the unit just made and D5 together **(5)**.

EYE PATCHES

Construct 2 triangle units – Sew A1 and C3 together **(6)**. Finish the left-facing eye patch – Sew 1 triangle unit, 1 eye unit, A3, A5, A6L, C7 and 2 pieces C5 in the order indicated **(7)**. Finish the right-facing eye patch – Sew 1 triangle unit, 1 eye unit, A3, A5, A6R, C7 and 2 pieces C5 in the order indicated **(8)**.

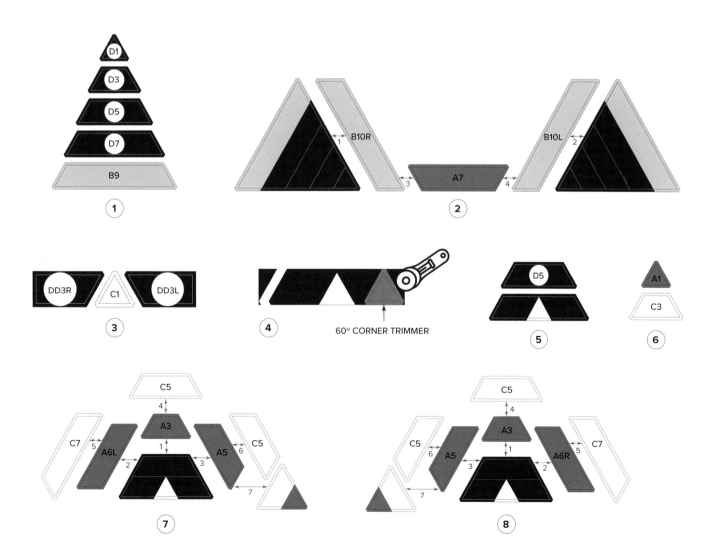

MUZZLE

Construct 1 nose unit – Sew C1, D3, C5 and C7 together **(9)**.

Construct 2 triangle units – Sew A1 and A3 together **(10)**. Finish the muzzle unit – Sew the nose unit, 2 pieces C7, 2 pieces B1, B11, 3 pieces B7, A5 and 2 triangle units together in the order indicated **(11)**.

FINAL ASSEMBLY AND QUILTING

Construct 2 triangle units – Sew A1 and A3 together **(10)**.

Construct 2 bottom ear units – Sew D1 and B3 together **(12)**. Sew A19, 2 pieces A3, A12L, A12R and all the

units you made together in the order indicated **(13)**. Press the seams in steps 4 and 5 and 8–11 to the shorter sides. Finish your rug without binding and quilt it as you like (see Useful Information: Rug Without Binding). Press your finished rug around the edges from the back side to help it lay flat. Add a non-slip backing if desired (see Additional Ideas).

WALL HANGING

Materials

A: 5 dark gray strips (2½in x WOF) or ½yd

B: 3 light gray strips (2½in x WOF) or ¼yd

C: 3 white strips (2½in x WOF) or ¼yd

D: 3 black strips (2½in x WOF) or ¼yd

E: 7 light blue strips (2½in x WOF) or ¾yd

Backing: 1½yd

Binding: 4 strips (2½in x WOF) or ½yd

Finished Size

43 x 26in

CUTTING FABRICS

Cut the shapes from fabrics A–D as described for the Area Rug, then cut the background pieces from fabric E as follows.

E Use 7 light blue strips (2½in x WOF)

E15 Cut 1 piece: 2½ x 19in; trim to create an isosceles trapezoid.

E13 Cut 1 piece: 2½ x 16¾in; trim to create an isosceles trapezoid.

E11 Cut 1 piece: 2½ x 14½in; trim to create an isosceles trapezoid.

E9 Cut 1 piece: 2½ x 12¼in; trim to create an isosceles trapezoid.

EE8R & EE8L Cut 2 pieces: 2½ x 11in; trim to create 1 right-leaning trapezoid and 1 left-leaning trapezoid.

E7 Cut 1 piece: 2½ x 9¾in; trim to create an isosceles trapezoid.

EE7R & EE7L Cut 2 pieces: 2½ x 9¾in; trim to create 1 right-leaning trapezoid and 1 left-leaning trapezoid.

EE6R & EE6L Cut 2 pieces: 2½ x 8¾in; trim to create 1 right-leaning trapezoid and 1 left-leaning trapezoid.

E5 Cut 1 piece: 2½ x 7½in; trim to create an isosceles trapezoid.

EE5R & EE5L Cut 6 pieces: 2½ x 7½in; trim to create 3 right-leaning trapezoids and 3 left-leaning trapezoids.

EE4R & EE4L Cut 6 pieces: 2½ x 6½in; trim to create 3 right-leaning trapezoids and 3 left-leaning trapezoids.

E3 Cut 3 pieces: 2½ x 5¼in; trim to create isosceles trapezoids.

E1 Cut 7 equilateral triangles.

PIECING AND QUILTING

Sew with a ¼in seam allowance,
pressing the seams open.

EARS
Construct 2 ear units – Same as for the Area Rug (1).

FACE
Construct 2 eyes, 2 eye patches and 1 muzzle
unit – Same as for the Area Rug (3–11). Finish
the face – Sew the muzzle unit, A19 and 2 eye
patches together in the order indicated, referring
to Area Rug diagram (13), steps 1–3 only.

FINAL ASSEMBLY
In the following instructions, when piecing the right
and left-leaning trapezoids, always align their 60° / 120°
corners and sew to the side with the right angles.

Construct 2 triangle units – Sew A1 and A3
together, referring to Area Rug diagram (10).

Construct 2 bottom ear units – Sew D1 and B3
together, referring to Area Rug diagram (12).

Construct the background units – Sew E9, E11,
E13 and E15 together; sew EE4L, EE5L, EE6L,
EE7L and EE8L together; sew EE4R, EE5R, EE6R,
EE7R and EE8R together; sew E1, E3, EE4R,
EE5R, EE5L and EE4L together; sew E1, E3,
EE4L, EE5L, EE5R and EE4R together (20).

Construct the additional background units – Sew
E1, E3, E5 and E7 together, then cut this unit in half
vertically (14–15); sew E1 and A12L together (16); sew
A12R and E1 together (17); sew E1 and A3 together
(18); sew A3 and E1 together (19). Sew the face unit,
A7, B10R, B10L and all the units you made together in
the order indicated (20). Square up the finished top.

QUILTING AND BINDING
Make a quilt sandwich and quilt it as you like (see Useful
Information). Bind your wall hanging using 4 strips 2½in x
WOF (see Useful Information: Binding Rectangular Quilts).
Add a few picture hanging strips to display the finished
piece on the wall (see Additional Ideas: Wall Hanging).

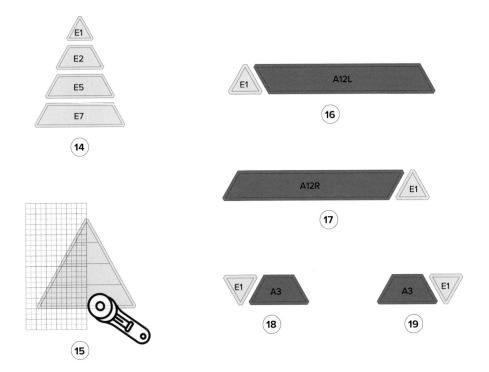

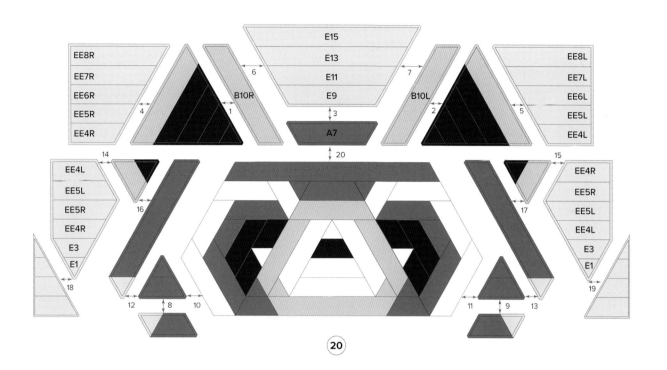

EE8R	EE8L
EE7R	EE7L
EE6R	EE6L
EE5R	EE5L
EE4R	EE4L

E15
E13
E11
E9
A7

B10R B10L

6 7 3 20

4 1 2 5

EE4L EE4R
EE5L EE5R
EE5R EE5L
EE4R EE4L
E3 E3
E1 E1

14 15 16 17 18 19

12 8 10 11 9 13

(20)

Quilt

Materials

A: 5 dark gray strips (2½in x WOF) or ½yd

B: 3 light gray strips (2½in x WOF) or ¼yd

C: 5 white strips (2½in x WOF) or ½yd

D: 5 black strips (2½in x WOF) or ½yd

E: 7 light blue strips (2½in x WOF) + 1½yd or 2¼yd in total

Backing: 3¾yd

Binding: 6 strips (2½in x WOF) or ½yd

Finished Size

52 x 60in

CUTTING FABRICS

Make 1 raccoon block as described for the Wall Hanging, leaving 2 white and 2 black strips. Then cut the additional fabric E pieces as follows.

E Use additional light blue fabric (1½yd)

Cut away selvages, then cut the following border pieces:

Horizontal Borders Cut 3 strips 10in x LOF.

Vertical Borders Cut 1 strip 4½in x LOF and sub-cut into 2 equal strips 4½in wide.

PIECING AND QUILTING

Sew with a ¼in seam allowance unless otherwise indicated, pressing the seams open.

BORDERS, QUILTING AND BINDING

Construct striped border – Place the 2 black and 2 white strips together in alternating order and sew them together along the long sides. Sub-cut the finished unit into 7 pieces 5½in wide; sew them together **(21–22)**.

Referring to Useful Information: Borders, trim the vertical borders to the height of the raccoon block and sew on at each side, steps 1 and 2 **(23)**. Trim the striped border and horizontal borders to the width of the raccoon block with attached vertical borders and sew them as indicated, steps 3–6 **(23)**.

Cut the backing fabric in half across WOF. Cut away selvages and sew 2 pieces together along the long sides with a ½in seam allowance; press the seam open. Make a quilt sandwich and quilt it as you like. Bind your quilt using 6 strips 2½in x WOF (see Useful Information: Binding Rectangular Quilts).

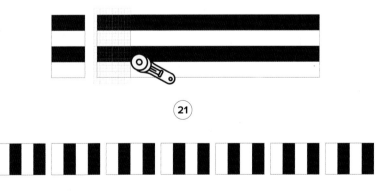

21

22

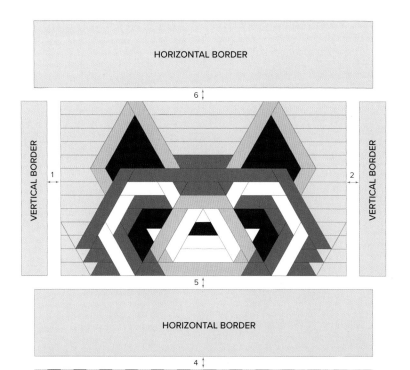

(23)

EXTRAS

BANNER

Construct 3 blue and 4 striped flag units referring to the triangular background unit from the Wall Hanging **(14)**. Position the striped and light blue flags in alternating order and rotate the striped flags. Finish the banner as described in Additional Ideas: Banner).

PLACEMAT

Sew 1 black and 1 white strip together, then sub-cut the finished unit into 5 pieces 5½in wide **(24)**; sew these pieces together, alternating black and white sections to create stripes **(25)**. Using 2 light blue strips (2½in x WOF), cut 4 pieces E-20½in (2½ x 20½in). Sew 2 pieces E-20½in together along the long sides twice, then sew these background units to the top and bottom edges of the striped unit **(26)**. Make a quilt sandwich and quilt it as you like (see Useful Information). Bind your placemat using 2 strips 2½in x WOF (see Useful Information: Binding Rectangular Quilts).

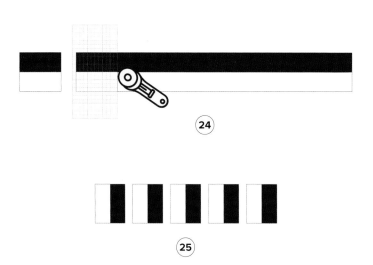

(24)

(25)

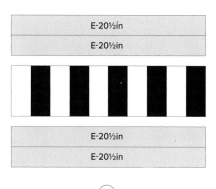

(26)

ARTFUL FOX

The artful fox quilt makes a wonderful gift, if you can bear to part with it, and is complemented by a matching rug that is sure to be admired. The quilt's pine tree motif can be used to make placemats, which are great for everyday use or for decorating your dining table for the holidays, and the pattern can easily be modified into a soft pillow for your couch. You can also finish a lovely forest banner for a woodland themed room by simply using the full border unit from the quilt.

This theme features Northcott Stonehenge Gradations Brights Strip Packs (Sunglow and Rainforest), as well as Stonehenge Gradations and Shimmer Radiance Single Colorway. Piecing and quilting are done using Aurifil 50wt cotton thread in coordinating colors.

Color Key

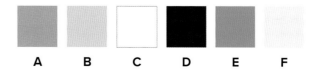

A   B   C   D   E   F

AREA RUG

Materials

A: 9 orange strips in various shades (2½in x WOF) or ¾yd

B: 2 yellow strips (2½in x WOF) or ¼yd

C: 4 white strips (2½in x WOF) or ½yd

D: 1 black strip (2½in x WOF) or fabric scraps

Backing: 1¼yd

Finished Size

41 x 28in

CUTTING FABRICS

A Use 9 orange strips (2½in x WOF)

A29in Cut 1 piece: 2½ x 35¼in; trim to create an isosceles trapezoid.

A16R & A16L Cut 2 pieces: 2½ x 20¼in; trim to create 1 right-leaning parallelogram and 1 left-leaning parallelogram.

A14R & A14L Cut 2 pieces: 2½ x 18in; trim to create 1 right-leaning parallelogram and 1 left-leaning parallelogram.

A13 Cut 1 piece: 2½ x 16¾in; trim to create an isosceles trapezoid.

A12R & A12L Cut 2 pieces: 2½ x 15½in; trim to create 1 right-leaning parallelogram and 1 left-leaning parallelogram.

A11 Cut 1 piece: 2½ x 14½in; trim to create an isosceles trapezoid.

A10R & A10L Cut 4 pieces: 2½ x 13¼in; trim to create 2 right-leaning parallelograms and 2 left-leaning parallelograms.

A9 Cut 4 pieces: 2½ x 12¼in; trim to create isosceles trapezoids.

A7 Cut 1 piece: 2½ x 9¾in; trim to create an isosceles trapezoid.

A5 Cut 1 piece: 2½ x 7½in; trim to create an isosceles trapezoid.

A3 Cut 3 pieces: 2½ x 5¼in; trim to create isosceles trapezoids.

A1 Cut 3 equilateral triangles.

B Use 2 yellow strips (2½in x WOF)

B7 Cut 2 pieces: 2½ x 9¾in; trim to create isosceles trapezoids.

B5 Cut 2 pieces: 2½ x 7½in; trim to create isosceles trapezoids.

B3 Cut 2 pieces: 2½ x 5¼in; trim to create isosceles trapezoids.

B1 Cut 4 equilateral triangles.

C Use 4 white strips (2½in x WOF)

C27 Cut 1 piece: 2½ x 33in; trim to create an isosceles trapezoid.

C-14½in Cut 2 pieces: 2½ x 14½in; trim each piece to 2 x 14½in.

C8R & C8L Cut 2 pieces: 2½ x 11in; trim to create 1 right-leaning parallelogram and 1 left-leaning parallelogram.

C7 Cut 2 pieces: 2½ x 9¾in; trim to create isosceles trapezoids.

C5 Cut 2 pieces: 2½ x 7½in; trim to create isosceles trapezoids.

C3 Cut 2 pieces: 2½ x 5¼in; trim to create isosceles trapezoids.

C-4in Cut 2 pieces: 2½ x 4in; sub-cut each piece into 2 rectangles 1 x 4in.

C1 Cut 2 equilateral triangles.

D Use 1 black strip (2½in x WOF)

D-7½in Cut 1 piece: 2½ x 7½in and sub-cut into 2 rectangles 1 x 7½in.

D3 Cut 1 piece: 2½ x 5¼in; trim to create an isosceles trapezoid.

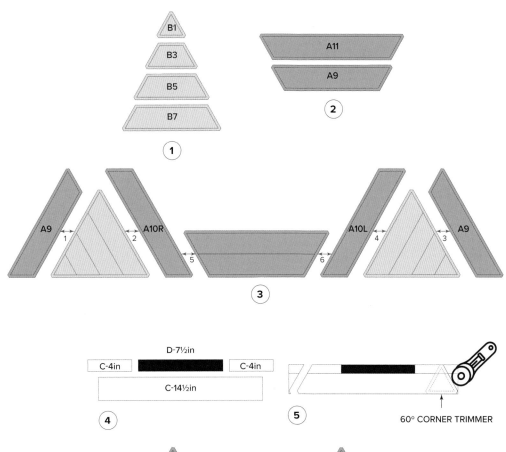

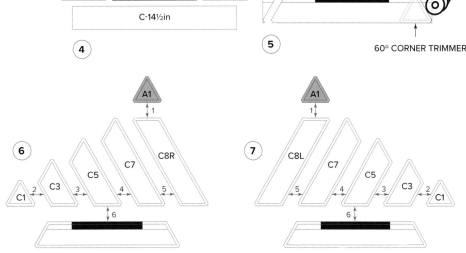

PIECING AND QUILTING

Sew with a ¼in seam allowance, pressing the seams open unless otherwise indicated.

EARS AND HEAD CROWN

Construct 2 ears – Sew B1, B3, B5 and B7 together **(1)**.

Construct 1 head crown – Sew A9 and A11 together **(2)**. Finish the unit – Sew 2 ears, head crown, A10R, A10L and 2 pieces A9 together in the order indicated **(3)**, pressing the seams to the center piece in steps 5 and 6.

EYES

Construct 2 eye units – Sew D-7½in and 2 pieces C-4in together, then sew C-14½in to the bottom of this unit **(4)**; with the black edge facing up, trim off the corners to create an isosceles trapezoid **(5)**.

EYE PATCHES

Construct 1 left-facing eye patch – Sew A1, C1, C3, C5, C7, C8R and 1 eye unit together in the order indicated **(6)**.

Construct 1 right-facing eye patch – Sew A1, C1, C3, C5, C7, C8L and 1 eye unit together in the order indicated **(7)**.

MUZZLE

Construct 1 unit – Sew A1, A3, A5, A7, A9, A10R, A10L and D3 together in the order indicated **(8)**.

FINAL ASSEMBLY AND QUILTING

Construct 2 bottom ear units – Sew B1 and A3 together **(9)**. Sew A13, C27, A29, A12L, A14L, A16L, A12R, A14R, A16R and all the units you made together in the order indicated **(10)**. Press the seams in steps 6–13 to the shorter sides. Finish your rug without binding and quilt it as you like (see Useful Information: Rug Without Binding). Press your finished rug around the edges from the back side to help it lay flat. Add a non-slip backing if desired (see Additional Ideas).

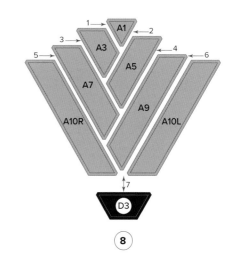

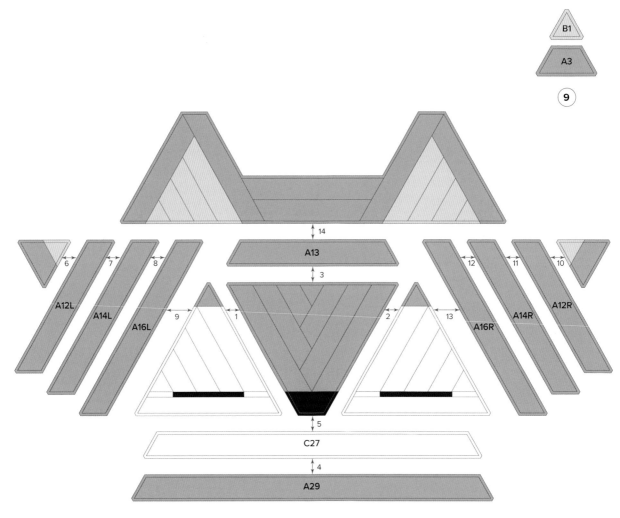

WALL HANGING

Materials

A: 9 orange strips in various shades (2½in x WOF) or ¾yd

B: 2 yellow strips (2½in x WOF) or ¼yd

C: 4 white strips (2½in x WOF) or ½yd

D: 1 black strip (2½in x WOF) or fabric scraps

F: 7 light neutral strips (2½in x WOF) or ¾yd

Backing: 1½yd

Binding: 4 strips (2½in x WOF) or ½yd

Finished Size

46 x 28in

CUTTING FABRICS

Cut the shapes from fabrics A–D as described for the Area Rug, then cut the background pieces from fabric F as follows.

F Use 7 light neutral strips (2½in x WOF)

F17 Cut 1 piece: 2½ x 21½in; trim to create an isosceles trapezoid.

F15 Cut 1 piece: 2½ x 19in; trim to create an isosceles trapezoid.

F13 Cut 1 piece: 2½ x 16¾in; trim to create an isosceles trapezoid.

F9 Cut 1 piece: 2½ x 12¼in; trim to create an isosceles trapezoid.

FF8R & FF8L Cut 2 pieces: 2½ x 11in; trim to create 1 right-leaning trapezoid and 1 left-leaning trapezoid.

F7 Cut 1 piece: 2½ x 9¾in; trim to create an isosceles trapezoid.

FF7R & FF7L Cut 2 pieces: 2½ x 9¾in; trim to create 1 right-leaning trapezoid and 1 left-leaning trapezoid.

FF6R & FF6L Cut 2 pieces: 2½ x 8¾in; trim to create 1 right-leaning trapezoid and 1 left-leaning trapezoid.

F5 Cut 1 piece: 2½ x 7½in; trim to create an isosceles trapezoid.

FF5R & FF5L Cut 6 pieces: 2½ x 7½in; trim to create 3 right-leaning trapezoids and 3 left-leaning trapezoids.

FF4R & FF4L Cut 6 pieces: 2½ x 6½in; trim to create 3 right-leaning trapezoids and 3 left-leaning trapezoids.

F3 Cut 3 pieces: 2½ x 5¼in; trim to create isosceles trapezoids.

F1 Cut 9 equilateral triangles.

PIECING AND QUILTING

Sew with a ¼in seam allowance, pressing the seams open.

EARS AND HEAD CROWN
Construct 2 ears and 1 head crown – Same as for the Area Rug **(1–2)**.

EYES, EYE PATCHES AND MUZZLE
Same as for the Area Rug **(4–8)**.

HEAD

Construct 2 bottom ear units – Sew B1 and A3 together, referring to Area Rug diagram **(9)**.

Construct 1 left-facing head unit – Sew F1 and A12L together (Row 1); sew F1 and A14L together (Row 2); sew F1 and A16L together (Row 3); sew these 3 rows together **(11)**.

Construct 1 right-facing head unit – Sew F1 and A12R together (Row 1); sew F1 and A14R together (Row 2); sew F1 and A16R together (Row 3); sew these 3 rows together **(12)**.

FINAL ASSEMBLY

In the following instructions, when piecing the right and left-leaning trapezoids, always align their 60° / 120° corners and sew to the side with the right angles.

Construct the background units – Sew F13, F15 and F17 together; sew FF4L, FF5L, FF6L, FF7L and FF8L together; sew FF4R, FF5R, FF6R, FF7R and FF8R together; sew F1, F3, FF4R, FF5R, FF5L and FF4L together; sew F1, F3, FF4L, FF5L, FF5R and FF4R together **(14)**.

Construct an additional background unit – Sew F1, F3, F5, F7 and F9 together, then cut this unit in half vertically **(13)**.

Sew A13, C27, A29, A10R, A10L, 2 pieces A9 and all the units you made together in the order indicated **(14)**. Square up the finished top.

QUILTING AND BINDING

Make a quilt sandwich and quilt it as you like (see Useful Information). Bind your wall hanging using 4 strips 2½in x WOF (see Useful Information: Binding Rectangular Quilts). Add a few picture hanging strips to display the finished piece on the wall (see Additional Ideas: Wall Hanging).

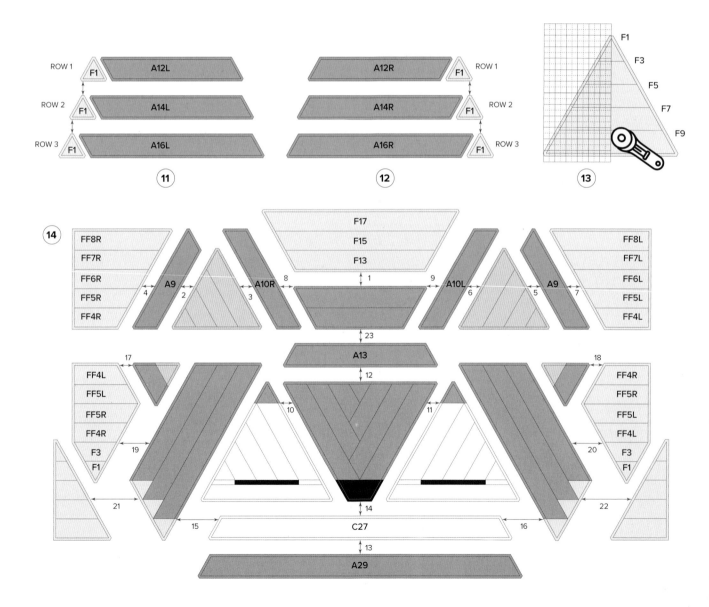

PLACEMAT

Materials

E: 2 green strips in different shades (2½in x WOF) or ¼yd

F: 3 light neutral strips (2½in x WOF) or ¼yd

Backing: 23 x 14in

Binding: 2 strips (2½in x WOF) or ¼yd

Finished Size

21 x 12in

CUTTING FABRICS

E Use 2 green strips (2½in x WOF)

E3 Cut 9 pieces: 2½ x 5¼in; trim to create isosceles trapezoids.

E1 Cut 3 equilateral triangles.

F Use 3 light neutral strips (2½in x WOF)

F-21in Cut 2 pieces: 2½ x 21in.

F5 Cut 2 pieces: 2½ x 7½in; trim to create isosceles trapezoids.

F3 Cut 6 pieces: 2½ x 5¼in; trim to create isosceles trapezoids.

FF3R & FF3L Cut 2 pieces: 2½ x 5¼in; trim to create 1 right-leaning trapezoid and 1 left-leaning trapezoid.

FF2R & FF2L Cut 6 pieces: 2½ x 4in; trim to create 3 right-leaning trapezoids and 3 left-leaning trapezoids.

PIECING AND QUILTING

Sew with a ¼in seam allowance, pressing the seams open.

FINAL ASSEMBLY, QUILTING AND BINDING

Construct Row 1 – Finish 3 treetops by sewing E1 and E3 together; finish 2 background units by sewing F3 and F5 together; sew FF2R and FF3R together; sew FF2L and FF3L together; sew the units you made together **(15)**.

Construct Rows 2 and 3 – Sew FF2R, FF2L, 3 pieces E3 and 2 pieces F3 together **(15)**. Sew Rows 1–3 together **(15)** and square up the block to 8½ x 21in.

Sew F-21in to the top and bottom edges of the block **(16)**. Make a quilt sandwich and quilt it as you like (see Useful Information). Bind your placemat using 2 strips 2½in x WOF (see Useful Information: Binding Rectangular Quilts).

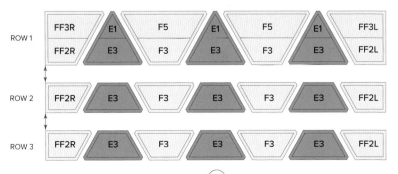

(15)

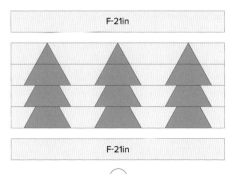

(16)

QuilT

Materials

A: 9 orange strips in various shades (2½in x WOF) or ¾yd

B: 2 yellow strips (2½in x WOF) or ¼yd

C: 4 white strips (2½in x WOF) or ½yd

D: 1 black strip (2½in x WOF) or fabric scraps

E: 4 green strips in various shades (2½in x WOF) or ½yd

F: 12 light neutral strips (2½in x WOF) + 1¾yd or 2¾yd in total

Backing: 3¾yd

Binding: 6 strips (2½in x WOF) or ½yd

Finished Size

55 x 60in

CUTTING FABRICS

Make 1 fox block as described for the Wall Hanging, then cut the additional pieces as follows.

E Use 4 green strips (2½in x WOF)

E3 Cut 21 pieces: 2½ x 5¼in; trim to create isosceles trapezoids.
E1 Cut 7 equilateral triangles.

F Use 5 light neutral strips (2½in x WOF)

FF6R & FF6L Cut 2 pieces: 2½ x 8¾in; trim to create 1 right-leaning trapezoid and 1 left-leaning trapezoid.
FF5R & FF5L Cut 6 pieces: 2½ x 7½in; trim to create 3 right-leaning trapezoids and 3 left-leaning trapezoids.
F5 Cut 6 pieces: 2½ x 7½in; trim to create isosceles trapezoids.
F3 Cut 18 pieces: 2½ x 5¼in; trim to create isosceles trapezoids.

F Use additional light neutral fabric (1¾yd)

Cut away selvages, then cut the following border pieces:
Wide Horizontal Borders Cut 2 strips 10in x LOF.
Narrow Horizontal Border Cut 1 strip 5in x LOF.
Vertical Borders Cut 1 strip 5in x LOF and sub-cut into 2 equal strips 5in wide.

PIECING AND QUILTING

Sew with a ¼in seam allowance unless otherwise indicated, pressing the seams open.

FOREST BORDER
Construct Row 1 – Finish 7 treetops by sewing E1 and E3 together **(17)**; finish 6 background units by sewing F3 and F5 together **(18)**; sew FF5R and FF6R together; sew FF5L and FF6L together; sew the units you made together **(19)**.

Construct Rows 2 and 3 – Sew FF5R, FF5L, 7 pieces E3 and 6 pieces F3 together **(19)**.

Sew Rows 1–3 together **(19)**.

FINAL ASSEMBLY
Referring to Useful Information: Borders, trim the edges of the vertical borders to the height of your fox block and sew them on each side, steps 1 and 2 **(20)**. Trim the edges of the forest border and all horizontal borders to the width of your fox block with vertical borders attached and sew them as indicated in steps 3–6 **(20)**.

QUILTING AND BINDING

Cut the backing fabric in half across WOF. Cut away selvages and sew 2 pieces together along the long sides with a ½in seam allowance; press the seam open. Make a quilt sandwich and quilt it as you like. Bind your quilt using 6 strips 2½in x WOF (see Useful Information: Binding Rectangular Quilts).

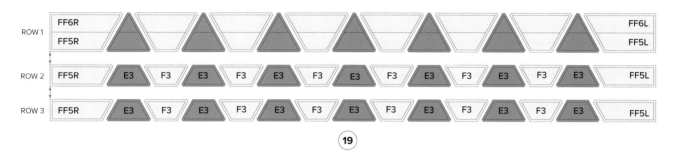

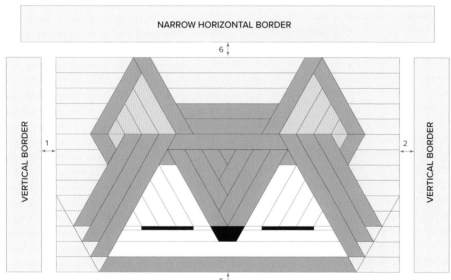

EXTRAS

BANNER

Make a matching banner for your woodland theme room using 4 green strips for the trees and 5 light neutral strips for the background. Construct 1 forest border as described for the Quilt **(17–19)**. Sub-cut this border into 7 flag units, cutting between the trees. Each finished flag unit should measure 8½in vertically and 7in horizontally after cutting. Finish the banner as described in Additional Ideas: Banner.

ENCHANTING ELEPHANT

Add a splash of color and transform your home into a magical place inspired by elephants, the most enchanting creatures in the animal kingdom. You can choose to make monochrome ears using four shades of your favorite color or create colorful ears in a rainbow gradient. Scrappy ears will also look fabulous if you wish to improvise using fabric strips from your Jelly Roll collection. Make a quilt, area rug, wall hanging and placemat, then complete a colorful banner and bed pillows using fabric leftovers. The wall hanging can also be used as a play mat for your little ones.

This theme features Dapple Pinwheel by Patrick Lose, Dapple Single Colorway and Northcott Canvas Single Colorway. Piecing and quilting are done using Aurifil 50wt cotton thread in coordinating colors.

Color key

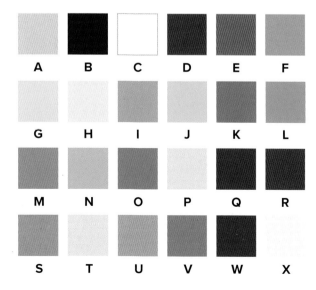

A	B	C	D	E	F
G	H	I	J	K	L
M	N	O	P	Q	R
S	T	U	V	W	X

AREA RUG

Materials

A: 11 medium gray strips (2½in x WOF) or 1yd

B: 1 black strip (2½in x WOF) or fabric scraps

C: 1 white strip (2½in x WOF) or fabric scraps

D–S: 16 colors of the rainbow, 2 strips of each color (2½in x WOF) or ¼yd of each color

Backing: 2yd

Finished Size

64 x 42in

CUTTING FABRICS

A Use 11 medium gray strips (2½in x WOF)

A-28¼in Cut 4 pieces: 2½ x 28¼in.

A23 Cut 1 piece: 2½ x 28¼in; trim to create an isosceles trapezoid.

A21 Cut 1 piece: 2½ x 26in; trim to create an isosceles trapezoid.

A19 Cut 1 piece: 2½ x 23¾in; trim to create an isosceles trapezoid.

A17 Cut 1 piece: 2½ x 21½in; trim to create an isosceles trapezoid.

A11 Cut 4 pieces: 2½ x 14½in; trim to create isosceles trapezoids.

A9 Cut 2 pieces: 2½ x 12¼in; trim to create isosceles trapezoids.

AA8L Cut 1 piece: 2½ x 11in; trim to create a left-leaning trapezoid.

AA7L Cut 1 piece: 2½ x 9¾in; trim to create a left-leaning trapezoid.

A7 Cut 1 piece: 2½ x 9¾in; trim to create an isosceles trapezoid.

A4R & A4L Cut 5 pieces: 2½ x 6½in; trim to create 4 right-leaning parallelograms and 1 left-leaning parallelogram.

A3 Cut 4 pieces: 2½ x 5¼in; trim to create isosceles trapezoids.

A2R & A2L Cut 2 pieces: 2½ x 4in; trim to create 1 right-leaning parallelogram and 1 left-leaning parallelogram.

A1 Cut 2 equilateral triangles.

B Use 1 black strip (2½in x WOF)

B3 Cut 2 pieces: 2½ x 5¼in; trim to create isosceles trapezoids.

B2R Cut 2 pieces: 2½ x 4in; trim to create 2 right-leaning parallelograms.

C Use 1 white strip (2½in x WOF)

C1 Cut 2 equilateral triangles.

D–S Use 16 colors of the rainbow, 2 strips of each color (2½in x WOF) / For monochrome ears, use fabrics T–W instead (see Wall Hanging)

D3 & S3 Using strips D and S, cut 6 pieces from each color: 2½ x 5¼in; trim to create isosceles trapezoids.

D1 & S1 Using strips D and S, cut 6 equilateral triangles from each color.

K3 & L3 Using strips K and L, cut 10 pieces from each color: 2½ x 5¼in; trim to create isosceles trapezoids.

K1 & L1 Using strips K and L, cut 10 equilateral triangles from each color.

E3–J3 & M3–R3 Using the remaining colors, cut 8 pieces from each color: 2½ x 5¼in; trim to create isosceles trapezoids.

E1–J1 & M1–R1 Using the remaining colors, cut 8 equilateral triangles from each color.

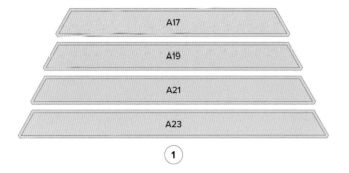

(1)

(2)

PIECING AND QUILTING

Sew with a ¼in seam allowance, pressing the seams open unless otherwise indicated.

HEAD CROWN AND FOREHEAD

Construct 1 head crown unit – Sew A17, A19, A21 and A23 together **(1)**.

Construct 1 forehead unit – Sew 4 pieces A-28¼in together **(2)**.

FACE

Sew A11, 2 pieces A3, 2 pieces B2R and 2 pieces C1 together (Row 1); sew A11, 2 pieces B3, A2L and A2R together (Row 2); sew A11, A9, A4L, A4R, 2 pieces A3 and 2 pieces A1 together in the order indicated (Row 3); sew these 3 rows together **(3)**.

TRUNK

Sew A11, A9, A7, 3 pieces A4R, AA8L and AA7L together in the order indicated **(4)**.

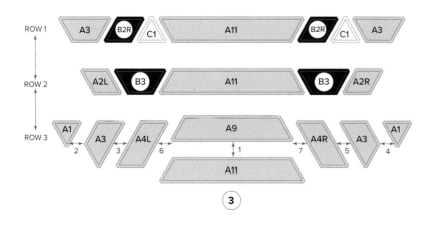

(3)

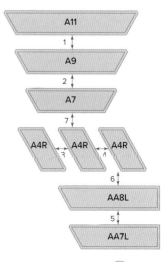

(4)

COLORFUL EARS

Construct 6 units D1 & D3, 6 units S1 & S3, 10 units K1 & K3, 10 units L1 & L3 and 8 units using each of the remaining colors (5). Using the units just made, construct 5 sections for the left and right-facing ears according to diagram (6); do not sew these sections together yet. Square up Section 3 of each ear, cutting ¼in away from the points for seam allowances (7).

FINAL ASSEMBLY AND QUILTING

Sew all the units together in the order indicated (8), pressing the trunk seam to the shorter side. Using a ruler with curved edges or a round plate, round up the points around the trunk and ears (8). Finish your rug without binding and quilt it as you like (see Useful Information: Rug Without Binding). Add a non-slip backing if desired (see Additional Ideas).

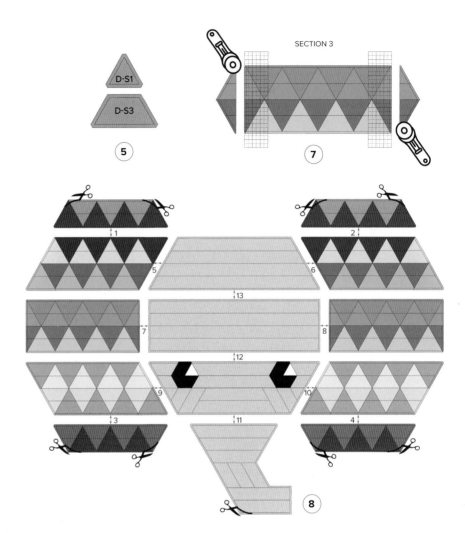

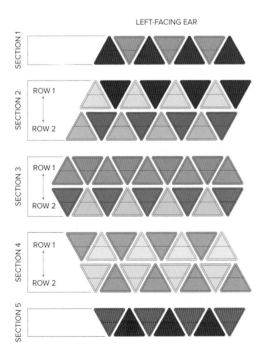

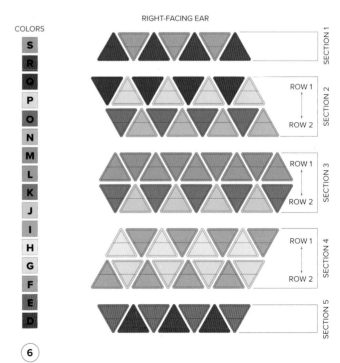

WALL HANGING

Materials

A: 11 medium gray strips (2½in x WOF) or 1yd

B: 1 black strip (2½in x WOF) or fabric scraps

C: 1 white strip (2½in x WOF) or fabric scraps

T, U, V, W: 4 shades of blue from light to dark, 7 strips of each shade (2½in x WOF) or ¾yd of each shade

X: 16 light neutral strips (2½in x WOF) or 1¼yd

Backing: 2½yd

Binding: 6 strips (2½in x WOF) or ½yd

Finished Size

69 x 42in

CUTTING FABRICS

Cut the shapes from fabrics A–C as described for the Area Rug, then cut the additional pieces as follows.

T, U, V, W Use 4 shades of blue from light to dark, 7 strips of each shade (2½in x WOF) / For colorful ears, use fabrics D–S instead (see Area Rug)

T3–W3 Cut 32 pieces from each color shade: 2½ x 5¼in; trim to create isosceles trapezoids.

T1–W1 Cut 32 equilateral triangles from each color shade.

X Use 16 light neutral strips (2½in x WOF)

XX30L Cut 1 piece: 2½ x 36½in; trim to create a left-leaning trapezoid.

XX29L Cut 1 piece: 2½ x 35¼in; trim to create a left-leaning trapezoid.

XX28L Cut 1 piece: 2½ x 34in; trim to create a left-leaning trapezoid.

XX27L Cut 1 piece: 2½ x 33in; trim to create a left-leaning trapezoid.

XX26R & XX26L Cut 3 pieces: 2½ x 31¾in; trim to create 1 right-leaning trapezoid and 2 left-leaning trapezoids.

XX25L Cut 1 piece: 2½ x 30½in; trim to create a left-leaning trapezoid.

X-26in Cut 2 pieces: 2½ x 26in.

X19 Cut 1 piece: 2½ x 23¾in; trim to create an isosceles trapezoid.

X17 Cut 1 piece: 2½ x 21½in; trim to create an isosceles trapezoid.

XX7R & XX7L Cut 4 pieces: 2½ x 9¾in; trim to create 2 right-leaning trapezoids and 2 left-leaning trapezoids.

XX6R & XX6L Cut 4 pieces: 2½ x 8¾in; trim to create 2 right-leaning trapezoids and 2 left-leaning trapezoids.

XX5R & XX5L Cut 4 pieces: 2½ x 7½in; trim to create 2 right-leaning trapezoids and 2 left-leaning trapezoids.

X5 Cut 2 pieces: 2½ x 7½in; trim to create isosceles trapezoids.

XX4R & XX4L Cut 4 pieces: 2½ x 6½in; trim to create 2 right-leaning trapezoids and 2 left-leaning trapezoids.

XX3R & XX3L Cut 4 pieces: 2½ x 5¼in; trim to create 2 right-leaning trapezoids and 2 left-leaning trapezoids.

X3 Cut 2 pieces: 2½ x 5¼in; trim to create isosceles trapezoids.

XX2R & XX2L Cut 4 pieces: 2½ x 4in; trim to create 2 right-leaning trapezoids and 2 left-leaning trapezoids.

X-3in Cut 8 pieces: 2½ x 3in.

PIECING AND QUILTING

Sew with a ¼in seam allowance unless otherwise indicated, pressing the seams open.

HEAD CROWN, FOREHEAD AND FACE
Same as for the Area Rug **(1–3)**.

TRUNK
Sew A11, A9, A7 together; sew 3 pieces A4R together; sew AA8L and AA7L together **(10)**. (Note: these 3 sections will be joined in the final assembly.)

MONOCHROME EARS
Using triangles and isosceles trapezoids from fabrics T–W, construct 32 units from each color shade as for the colorful ears of the Area Rug **(5)**. Using the units just made, construct 5 sections for the left and right-facing ears according to diagram **(9)**; do not sew these sections together yet. Square up Section 3 of each ear as for the colorful ears of the Area Rug, cutting ¼in away from the points for seam allowances **(7)**.

To make colorful ears, refer to color layout for Area Rug (5–7).

LEFT-FACING EAR

COLORS

| T |
| U |
| V |
| W |

RIGHT-FACING EAR

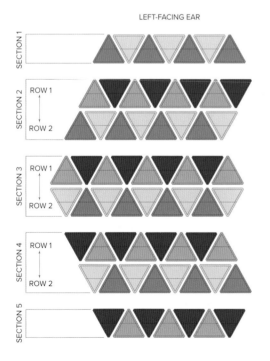

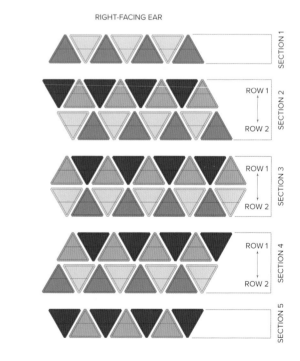

SECTION 1

SECTION 2 — ROW 1 / ROW 2

SECTION 3 — ROW 1 / ROW 2

SECTION 4 — ROW 1 / ROW 2

SECTION 5

9

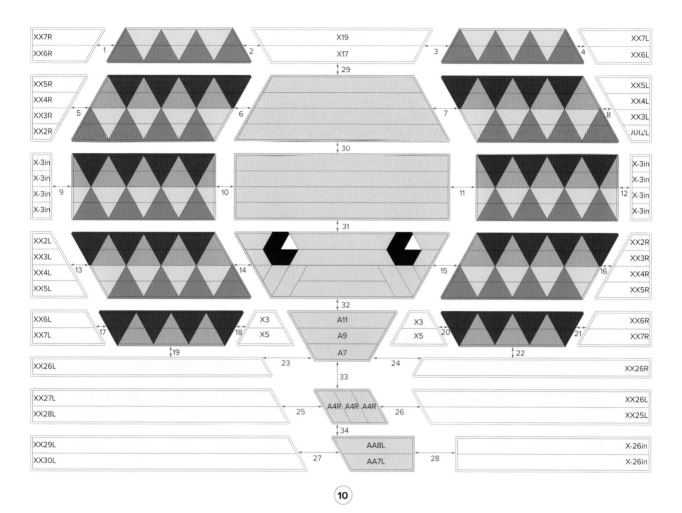

(10)

FINAL ASSEMBLY

In the following instructions, when piecing the right and left-leaning trapezoids, always align their 60° / 120° corners and sew to the side with the right angles.

Construct the background units – Sew X17 and X19 together; sew X3 and X5 together twice; sew XX6R and XX7R together twice; sew XX6L and XX7L together twice; sew XX2R, XX3R, XX4R and XX5R together twice; sew XX2L, XX3L, XX4L and XX5L together twice; sew 4 pieces X-3in together twice; sew XX25L and XX26L together; sew XX27L and XX28L together; sew XX29L and XX30L together; sew 2 pieces X-26in together **(10)**.

Sew all the units together in the order indicated **(10)**. When sewing rows (steps 29–34), align all intersecting points using pins and do not worry about matching up the side edges. Square up the finished top.

QUILTING AND BINDING

Cut the backing fabric in half across WOF. Cut away selvages and sew 2 pieces together along the long sides with a ½in seam allowance; press the seam open. Make a quilt sandwich and quilt it as you like (see Useful Information). Bind your wall hanging using 6 strips 2½in x WOF (see Useful Information: Binding Rectangular Quilts). Add a few picture hanging strips to display the finished piece on the wall (see Additional Ideas: Wall Hanging).

QUILT

Materials

A: 11 medium gray strips (2½in x WOF) or 1yd

B: 1 black strip (2½in x WOF) or fabric scraps

C: 1 white strip (2½in x WOF) or fabric scraps

D–S: 16 colors of the rainbow, 1 strip of each color (2½in x WOF) or fabric scraps

T, U, V, W: 4 shades of blue from light to dark, 7 strips of each shade (2½in x WOF) or ¾yd of each shade

X: 17 light neutral strips (2½in x WOF) + 1¾yd or 3yd in total

Backing: 5yd

Binding: 8 strips (2½in x WOF) or ¾yd

Finished Size

69 x 80in

CUTTING FABRICS

Make 1 elephant block as described for the Wall Hanging, then cut the additional pieces as follows.

D–S Use 16 colors of the rainbow, 1 strip of each color (2½in x WOF)

DD3R & DD3L Using strip D, cut 4 pieces: 2½ x 5¼in; trim to create 2 right-leaning trapezoids and 2 left-leaning trapezoids.

DD2R & DD2L Using strip D, cut 4 pieces: 2½ x 4in; trim to create 2 right-leaning trapezoids and 2 left-leaning trapezoids.

E3–S3 Using remaining colors, cut 4 pieces from each color: 2½ x 5¼in; trim to create isosceles trapezoids.

E1–S1 Using remaining colors, cut 4 equilateral triangles from each color.

X Use 1 light neutral strip (2½in x WOF)

XX3R & XX3L Cut 4 pieces: 2½ x 5¼in; trim to create 2 right-leaning trapezoids and 2 left-leaning trapezoids.

XX2R & XX2L Cut 4 pieces: 2½ x 4in; trim to create 2 right-leaning trapezoids and 2 left-leaning trapezoids.

X Use additional light neutral fabric (1¾yd)

Horizontal Borders Cut 4 strips 6in x WOF.

Filler Blocks Cut away selvages, then cut 2 pieces 19½in x LOF.

PIECING AND QUILTING

Sew with a ¼in seam allowance unless otherwise indicated, pressing the seams open.

COLORFUL BORDER
Construct 2 borders. For side units, sew DD3R to DD2R; DD3L to DD2L; XX3R to XX2R; XX3L to XX2L **(11)**.

Construct triangle units as in diagram **(5)** of the Area Rug, using E–S shapes. Finish 2 rows as in diagram **(11)**. Sew Row 1 and Row 2 together. Square up the finished border unit.

FINAL ASSEMBLY
Trim edges of horizontal borders to the width of the colorful borders and sew to top and bottom edges; then sew a filler block to the side of each border, steps 1–6 **(12)**. Trim the finished borders to the width of the elephant block and sew to top and bottom edges, steps 7 and 8 **(12)**.

QUILTING AND BINDING
Cut the backing fabric in half across WOF. Cut away selvages and sew 2 pieces together along the long sides with a ½in seam allowance; press the seam open. Make a quilt sandwich and quilt it as you like. Bind your quilt using 8 strips 2½in x WOF (see Useful Information: Binding Rectangular Quilts).

ROW 1

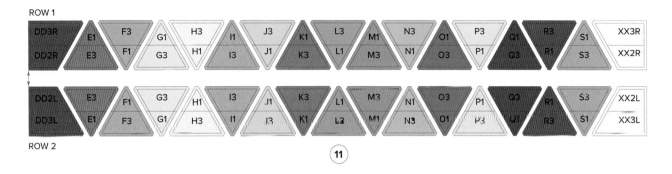

ROW 2

(11)

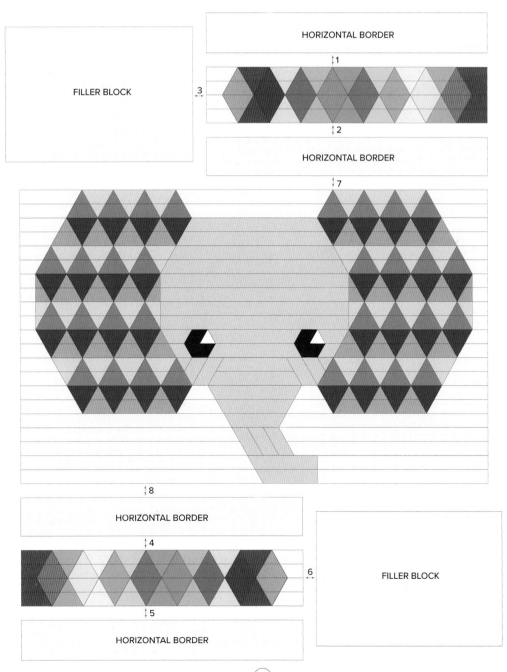

FILLER BLOCK

HORIZONTAL BORDER

↕1

3

↕2

HORIZONTAL BORDER

↕7

↕8

HORIZONTAL BORDER

↕4

6

↕5

FILLER BLOCK

HORIZONTAL BORDER

(12)

PLACEMAT

Materials

T, U, V, W: 4 shades of blue from light to dark, 1 strip of each shade (2½in x WOF) or fabric scraps

X: 2 light neutral strips (2½in x WOF) or ¼yd

Backing: 21 x 14in

Binding: 2 strips (2½in x WOF) or ¼yd

Finished Size

19 x 12in

CUTTING FABRICS

T, U, V, W Use 4 shades of blue from light to dark, 1 strip of each shade (2½in x WOF)

TT3R & UU3L Using strips T and U, cut 1 piece from each strip holding them with wrong sides together: 2½ x 5¼in; trim to create 1 right-leaning trapezoid and 1 left-leaning trapezoid.

TT2R & UU2L Using strips T and U, cut 1 piece from each strip holding them with wrong sides together: 2½ x 4in; trim to create 1 right-leaning trapezoid and 1 left-leaning trapezoid.

T3–W3 Cut 2 pieces from strips T and U and 3 pieces from strips V and W: 2½ x 5¼in; trim to create isosceles trapezoids.

T1–W1 Cut 2 equilateral triangles from strips T and U and 3 equilateral triangles from strips V and W.

X Use 2 light neutral strips (2½in x WOF)

X-19in Cut 2 pieces: 2½ x 19in.

XX3R & XX3L Cut 2 pieces: 2½ x 5¼in; trim to create 1 right-leaning trapezoid and 1 left-leaning trapezoid.

XX2R & XX2L Cut 2 pieces: 2½ x 4in; trim to create 1 right-leaning trapezoid and 1 left-leaning trapezoid.

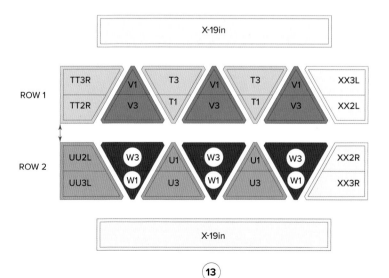

EXTRAS

PIECING AND QUILTING

Sew with a ¼in seam allowance, pressing the seams open.

FINAL ASSEMBLY

Construct 2 rows according to diagram and sew these rows together **(13)**. Sew X-19in to the top and bottom edges and square up the finished block **(13)**.

QUILTING AND BINDING

Make a quilt sandwich and quilt it as you like (see Useful Information). Bind your placemat using 2 strips 2½in x WOF (see Useful Information: Binding Rectangular Quilts).

PILLOWCASE

You will need colorful or monochrome fabric scraps for the center unit, ¾yd of background fabric, plus fabrics for backing and binding. Simply turn the placemat block **(13)** into a pillowcase by adding background fabrics around the edges to the desired size. If you wish, you can use colorful strips D–S in place of monochrome fabrics T–W and follow the color layout of the quilt border **(11)**. Finish your pillowcase as described in Additional Ideas: Pillowcase.

BANNER

The banner is made from fabric leftovers. Using colorful fabric strips D–S, construct 6–7 flags using triangle units from the quilt border. You will need 4 triangle units **(5)** to construct each flag **(14)**, following the color layout shown in the quilt border **(11)**. Each finished flag measures 8in vertically and 9in horizontally, so you can estimate the length for your banner. Finish the banner as described in Additional Ideas: Banner.

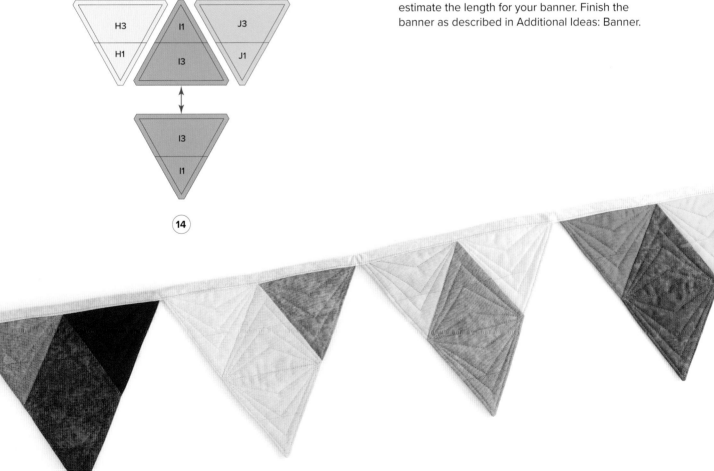

14

LUCKY LADYBUG

On a bright summer morning, wrap up in your lucky ladybug quilt to sip some tea and feel as snug as a bug in a rug. Make a daisy placemat for your morning beverage and a sweet ladybug rug to keep your toes chic and cozy. Ladybugs will protect your flowers on the quilt and in the garden, so you can dress up your patio with a floral banner and make a matching comfy pillow using motifs from the placemat pattern.

This theme features Basically Black and White Pinwheel by Patrick Lose and Mixmasters Mashup Single Colorway by Patrick Lose. Piecing and quilting are done using Aurifil 50wt cotton thread in coordinating colors.

Color key

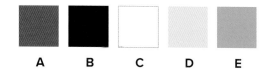

A   B   C   D   E

AREA RUG

Materials

A: 6 red strips (2½in x WOF) or ½yd

B: 5 black strips (2½in x WOF) + ½yd for bias tape or 1yd in total

C: 1 white strip (2½in x WOF) or fabric scraps

Backing: ¾yd

Finished Size

32 x 20in

CUTTING FABRICS

A Use 6 red strips (2½in x WOF)

AA6R & AA6L Cut 6 pieces: 2½ x 8¾in; trim to create 3 right-leaning trapezoids and 3 left-leaning trapezoids.

AA5R & AA5L Cut 2 pieces: 2½ x 7½in; trim to create 1 right-leaning trapezoid and 1 left-leaning trapezoid.

A5 Cut 14 pieces: 2½ x 7½in; trim to create isosceles trapezoids.

A3 Cut 2 pieces: 2½ x 5¼in; trim to create isosceles trapezoids.

A2R & A2L Cut 2 pieces: 2½ x 4in; trim to create 1 right-leaning parallelogram and 1 left-leaning parallelogram.

AA2R & AA2L Cut 4 pieces: 2½ x 4in; trim to create 2 right-leaning trapezoids and 2 left-leaning trapezoids.

A1 Cut 2 equilateral triangles.

B Use 5 black strips (2½in x WOF)

B13 Cut 1 piece: 2½ x 16¾in; trim to create an isosceles trapezoid.

B9 Cut 2 pieces: 2½ x 12¼in; trim to create isosceles trapezoids.

B3 Cut 24 pieces: 2½ x 5¼in; trim to create isosceles trapezoids.

C Use 1 white strip (2½in x WOF)

C1 Cut 2 equilateral triangles.

PIECING AND QUILTING

Sew with a ¼in seam allowance, pressing the seams open unless otherwise indicated.

BODY
Construct the top of the body – Sew A2R, 2 pieces B3, A5 and AA6L together (Row 1); sew A3, 2 pieces B3, A5 and AA6R together (Row 2); sew 3 pieces B3, 2 pieces A5 and AA2L together (Row 3); sew A1, 3 pieces B3, 2 pieces A5 and AA2R together (Row 4); sew these 4 rows together, pinning their intersecting points **(1)**. Don't worry if the sides with the right angles do not match up perfectly as they will be trimmed later.

Construct the bottom of the body – Sew A2L, 2 pieces B3, A5 and AA6R together (Row 1); sew A3, 2 pieces B3, A5 and AA6L together (Row 2); sew 3 pieces B3, 2 pieces A5 and AA2R together (Row 3); sew A1, 3 pieces B3, 2 pieces A5 and AA2L together (Row 4); sew these 4 rows together, pinning their intersecting points **(2)**. Don't worry if the sides with the right angles do not match up perfectly as they will be trimmed later.

Construct the center of the body – Sew AA5R, 2 pieces B3, A5 and AA6L together (Row 1); sew AA5L, 2 pieces B3, A5 and AA6R together (Row 2); sew these 2 rows together and label the left side as Back Edge using masking tape **(3)**. This will help you prevent flipping the center piece upside down by accident.

HEAD

Construct 1 unit – Sew B13, 2 pieces C1 and 2 pieces B9 together in the order indicated **(4)**.

BODY DIVIDER AND ANTENNAE

Using ½yd of black fabric, cut 5 strips at a 45° angle 2in wide. You will be using 3 of these bias-cut strips for the body divider and 2 strips for the antennae.

Complete 1 body divider – Sew 3 bias-cut strips together. Using a bias maker, fold and press the long raw edges so that they meet in the center.

Complete 2 antennae – Using a bias maker, fold and press the long raw edges of both remaining bias-cut strips so that they meet in the center, then fold each strip along the center and press again. Topstitch from end to end along the first folds. Tie a knot on one side of each strip and trim away the point above the knot. Trim the other end of each strip to measure 5in before the knot.

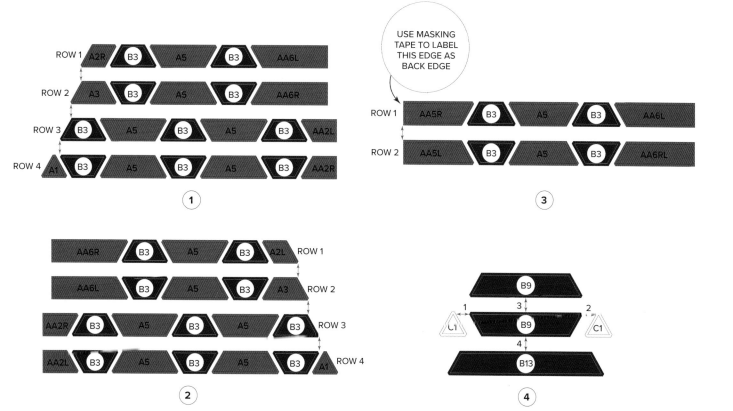

FINAL ASSEMBLY AND QUILTING

Position the body divider along the center of the body and topstitch around; trim away the overlapped ends on each side in step 1 **(5)**. Sew the top and bottom pieces of the body to the center piece in steps 2 and 3, aligning their pointy edges with the back edge of the center piece **(5)**. Square up the right side of the body (front edge). Fold the head in half to determine the center and sew it to the body, pressing the seam towards the head in step 4 **(5)**.

Position and pin the antennae on each side of the head, about 1in away and parallel to the side edges; the knots should be facing towards the body and the trimmed edges extending beyond the head edge by 1in **(6–7)**. Using a ruler with curved edges or a small round plate, round up the points around the ladybug **(6)**. Finish your rug without binding and quilt it as you like (see Useful Information: Rug Without Binding). Add a non-slip backing if desired (see Additional Ideas).

To add extra interest to your project, use fabric scraps with assorted red prints or combine a few shades of red for the ladybug's body.

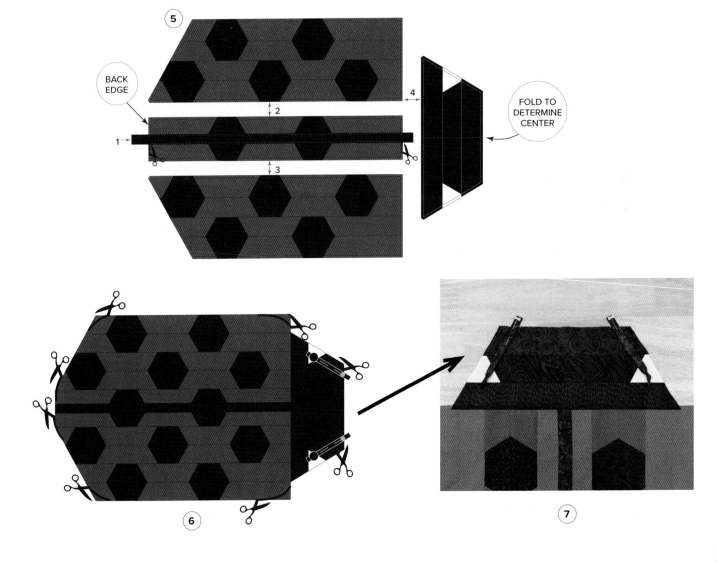

WALL HANGING

Materials

A: 6 red strips (2½in x WOF) or ½yd

B: 5 black strips (2½in x WOF) + ½yd for bias tape or 1yd in total

C: 1 white strip (2½in x WOF) or fabric scraps

E: 6 green strips (2½in x WOF) or ½yd

Backing: ¾yd

Binding: 4 strips (2½in x WOF) or ½yd

Finished Size

39 x 24in

CUTTING FABRICS

Cut the shapes from fabrics A–C as described for the Area Rug, then cut the background pieces from fabric E as follows.

E Use 6 green strips (2½in x WOF)

E-26in Cut 2 pieces: 2½ x 26in.

EE6R & EE6L Cut 2 pieces: 2½ x 8¾in; trim to create 1 right-leaning trapezoid and 1 left-leaning trapezoid.

EE5R & EE5L Cut 4 pieces: 2½ x 7½in; trim to create 2 right-leaning trapezoids and 2 left-leaning trapezoids.

EE4R & EE4L Cut 4 pieces: 2½ x 6½in; trim to create 2 right-leaning trapezoids and 2 left-leaning trapezoids.

EE3R & EE3L Cut 2 pieces: 2½ x 5¼in; trim to create 1 right-leaning trapezoid and 1 left-leaning trapezoid.

EE2R & EE2L Cut 2 pieces: 2½ x 4in; trim to create 1 right-leaning trapezoid and 1 left-leaning trapezoid.

E-3in Cut 2 pieces: 2½ x 3in.

Keep the remaining 2 strips uncut and set aside; they will be used as borders in Final Assembly.

PIECING AND QUILTING

Sew with a ¼in seam allowance, pressing the seams open.

BODY AND HEAD
Same as for the Area Rug **(1–4)**.

BODY DIVIDER AND ANTENNAE
Same as for the Area Rug: Body Divider and Antennae.

FINAL ASSEMBLY
In the following instructions, when piecing the right and left-leaning trapezoids, always align their 60° / 120° corners and sew to the side with the right angles.

Finish the head block – Sew EE6R, EE5R and EE4R together; sew EE6L, EE5L and EE4L together; sew these 2 background units to the head unit **(8)**. Position and pin the antennae on each side of the head along the head seams, knots facing towards the body and trimmed edges extending beyond the head edge by 1in **(9–10)**. Sew 2 pieces E-26in together, then sew this background unit to the front of the head, sandwiching the antennae between the layers **(9)**. Press the seam open, allowing each antenna to lean forward on the front side (longer ends with knots) and to lean backwards on the back side (shorter ends). Secure each antenna to the background by stitching a rectangle about 1in long and then stitch an "X" between the corners inside the rectangle **(11)**.

Finish the body block – Position the body divider along the center of the body and topstitch around; trim away the overlapped ends on each side in step 1 **(12)**. Sew 2 pieces E-3in together, then sew this background unit to the back edge of the center piece in step 2 **(12)**. Sew EE5R, EE4R, EE3R and EE2R together, then sew this background unit to the top part of the body in step 3 **(12)**. Sew EE5L, EE4L, EE3L and EE2L together, then sew this background unit to the bottom part of the body in step 4 **(12)**. Sew all the body units together in steps 5 and 6 and square up the block **(12)**. Trim the edges of the 2 set aside green border strips to the width of the body block and sew them to the top and bottom edges in steps 7 and 8 **(12)**.

Trim the edges of the head block to match the body block and sew these 2 blocks together in steps 9–11 **(12)**.

QUILTING AND BINDING

Make a quilt sandwich and quilt it as you like. Bind your wall hanging using 4 strips 2½in x WOF (see Useful Information). Add a few picture hanging strips to display (see Additional Ideas: Wall Hanging).

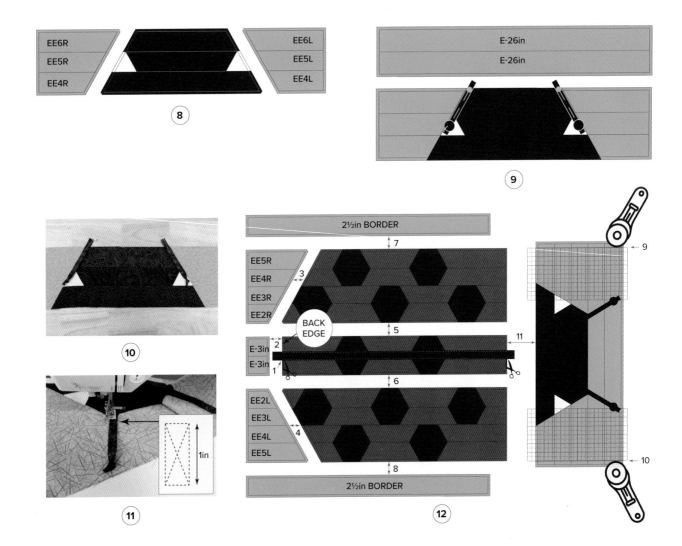

PLACEMAT

Materials

C: 2 white strips (2½in x WOF) or ¼yd

D: 1 yellow strip (2½in x WOF)

E: 3 green or blue strips (2½in x WOF) or ¼yd

Backing: 22 x 14in

Binding: 2 strips (2½in x WOF) or ¼yd

Finished Size

20 x 12in

CUTTING FABRICS

C Use 2 white strips (2½in x WOF)

C3 Cut 12 pieces: 2½ x 5¼in; trim to create isosceles trapezoids.

D Use 1 yellow strip (2½in x WOF)

D3 Cut 2 pieces: 2½ x 5¼in; trim to create isosceles trapezoids.

E Use 3 green or blue strips (2½in x WOF)

E-12½in Cut 2 pieces: 2½ x 12½in.

EE5R & EE5L Cut 4 pieces: 2½ x 7½in; trim to create 2 right-leaning trapezoids and 2 left-leaning trapezoids.

EE2R & EE2L Cut 8 pieces: 2½ x 4in; trim to create 4 right-leaning trapezoids and 4 left-leaning trapezoids.

PIECING AND QUILTING

Sew with a ¼in seam allowance, pressing the seams open.

FLOWER BLOCK

Construct Rows 1 and 6 – Sew EE5R, C3 and EE5L together **(13)**.

Construct Rows 2 and 5 – Sew EE2R, 3 pieces C3 and EE2L together **(13)**.

Construct Rows 3 and 4 – Sew EE2L, C3, D3, C3 and EE2R together **(13)**. Sew these 6 rows together **(13)**. When sewing rows, align all the intersecting points using pins and do not worry about matching up the side edges. Square up the finished block.

FINAL ASSEMBLY, QUILTING AND BINDING

Sew E-12½in pieces to the flower block **(14)**. Make a quilt sandwich and quilt it as you like. Bind the placemat using 2 strips 2½in x WOF (see Useful Information: Binding Rectangular Quilts).

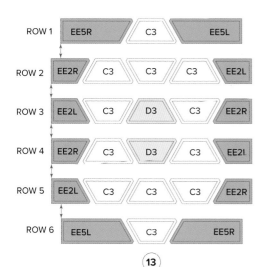

(13)

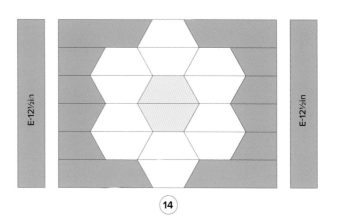

(14)

Quilt

Materials

A: 12 red strips (2½in x WOF) or 1yd

B: 9 black strips (2½in x WOF) + ½yd for bias tape or 1¼yd in total

C: 4 white strips (2½in x WOF) or ½yd

D: 1 yellow strip (2½in x WOF) or fabric scraps

E: 16 green strips (2½in x WOF) + 1¾yd or 3¼yd in total

Backing: 4½yd

Binding: 7 strips (2½in x WOF) or ¾yd

Finished Size

59 x 74in

CUTTING FABRICS

Make 2 ladybug blocks as described for the Wall Hanging. Make 2 flower blocks as described for the Placemat, omitting the E-12½in borders. Then cut the additional fabric F pieces as follows.

E Use additional green fabric (1¾yd)

Cut away selvages, then cut the following background pieces:

Horizontal Borders Cut 3 strips 9in x LOF.

Filler Blocks and Sashing Cut 1 strip 12½in x LOF; sub-cut into 2 filler blocks 21 x 12½in, and 2 sashing strips 12½ x 4½in.

PIECING AND QUILTING

Sew with a ¼in seam allowance unless otherwise indicated, pressing the seams open.

FLOWER UNITS

Construct 2 units – Sew a sashing strip to the right edge of a flower block, then trim a filler block to the same width and sew it to the bottom edge **(15)**.

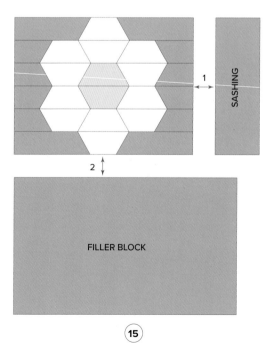

15

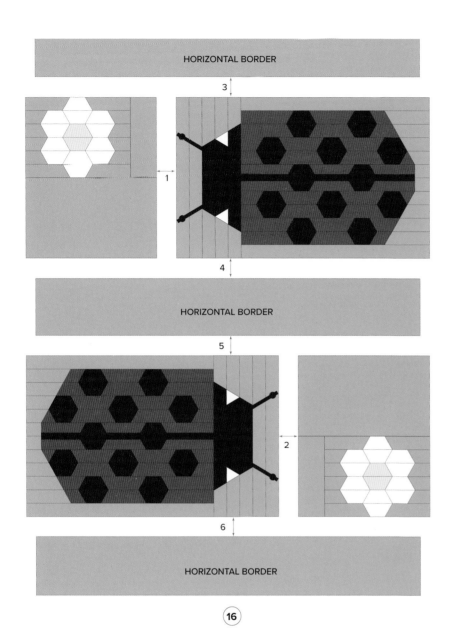

EXTRAS

PILLOWCASE

You will need fabric strips required for the placemat plus additional background fabric, and fabrics for backing and binding. To complete the top, simply follow the placemat pattern, then add borders from your additional background fabric to make it square. Finish your pillowcase as described in Additional Ideas: Pillowcase.

BANNER

You will need 1 yellow and 5 white strips plus fabrics for backing and binding. Construct 5–6 flag units referring to Rows 4–6 of the flower block and omitting its background pieces to make a half flower **(13)**. Each half-flower unit measures 6in vertically and 11in horizontally, so you can estimate the length for your banner. Finish the banner as described in Additional Ideas: Banner.

FINAL ASSEMBLY
Sew the flower units and ladybug blocks together as indicated in steps 1 and 2 **(16)**. Referring to Useful Information: Borders, trim the edges of all horizontal borders to the width of the finished units. Sew the units and borders together as indicated in steps 3–6 **(16)**.

QUILTING AND BINDING
Cut the backing fabric in half across WOF. Cut away selvages and sew 2 pieces together along the long sides with a ½in seam allowance; press the seam open. Make a quilt sandwich and quilt it as you like (see Useful Information). Bind your quilt using 7 strips 2½in x WOF (see Useful Information: Binding Rectangular Quilts).

SiNGiNG FROG

Whether in your home or on the go, at a picnic, camping or on a cottage trip, this frog quilt is as charming as it is cute. After a day spent in the great outdoors, wrap yourself up in it to enjoy a bonfire by the lake and the serenading frogs. Make an area rug for your cabin and set your table with matching placemats when you invite your friends to the party. To complete your cozy set up, whip up a welcoming banner and a few comfy pillows.

This theme features Northcott Stonehenge Gradations Strip Packs (Rainforest, Onyx and Iron Ore), as well as Stonehenge Gradations and Shimmer Radiance Single Colorway. Piecing and quilting are done using Aurifil 50wt cotton thread in coordinating colors.

Color key

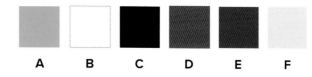

A B C D E F

AREA RUG

Materials

A: 10 green strips (2½in x WOF) or ¾yd

B: 2 white strips (2½in x WOF) or ¼yd

C: 1 black strip (2½in x WOF) or fabric scraps

D: 1 red strip (2½in x WOF) or ¼yd

Backing: 1yd

Finished Size

39 x 26in

CUTTING FABRICS

A Use 10 green strips (2½in x WOF)

A-39¾in Cut 1 piece: 2½ x 39¾in and sub-cut into 2 rectangles 1¼ x 39¾in.

A33 Cut 2 pieces: 2½ x 39¾in; trim to create isosceles trapezoids.

A31 Cut 2 pieces: 2½ x 37½in; trim to create isosceles trapezoids.

A29 Cut 2 pieces: 2½ x 35¼in; trim to create isosceles trapezoids.

A15 Cut 1 piece: 2½ x 19in; trim to create an isosceles trapezoid.

A6R & A6L Cut 8 pieces: 2½ x 8¾in; trim to create 4 right-leaning parallelograms and 4 left-leaning parallelograms.

A3 Cut 4 pieces: 2½ x 5¼in; trim to create isosceles trapezoids.

B Use 2 white strips (2½in x WOF)

B4R & B4L Cut 8 pieces: 2½ x 6½in; trim to create 4 right-leaning parallelograms and 4 left-leaning parallelograms.

B1 Cut 4 equilateral triangles.

C Use 1 black strip (2½in x WOF)

C3 Cut 4 pieces: 2½ x 5¼in; trim to create isosceles trapezoids.

D Use 1 red strip (2½in x WOF)

D-39¾in Cut 1 piece: 2½ x 39¾in and trim it to 1 x 39¾in.

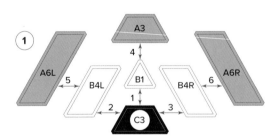

PIECING AND QUILTING

Sew with a ¼in seam allowance, pressing the seams open unless otherwise indicated.

EYES
Construct 4 units – Sew C3, B1, B4L, B4R, A3, A6L and A6R together in the order indicated **(1)**.

MOUTH
Construct 1 unit – Sew D-39¾in and 2 pieces A-39¾in together **(2)**.

FINAL ASSEMBLY AND QUILTING
Sew 4 eye units, mouth unit, A15, 2 pieces A29, 2 pieces A31 and 2 pieces A33 together in the order indicated **(3)**. Press the seams in steps 3 and 4 to the center piece. Using a ruler with curved edges or a small round plate, round up the points around the frog **(4)**. Finish your rug without binding and quilt it as you like (see Useful Information: Rug Without Binding). Add a non-slip backing if desired (see Additional Ideas).

> To cut a strip that is longer than your 36in cutting mat, fold your strip in half and measure 20in from the fold to cut a 40in strip, then trim away the excess to the specified length. Use pins when sewing long strips together.

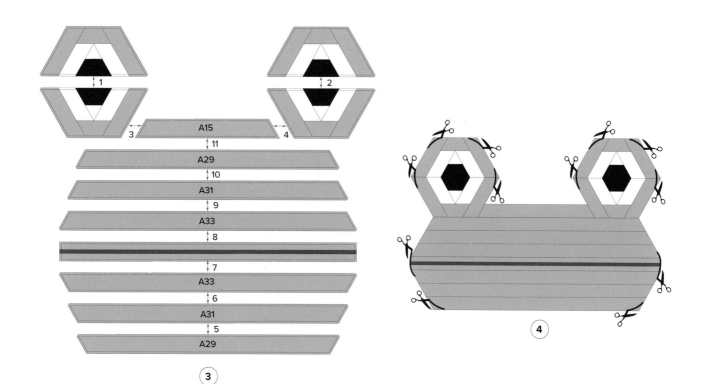

WALL HANGING

Materials

A: 10 green strips (2½in x WOF) or ¾yd

B: 2 white strips (2½in x WOF) or ¼yd

C: 1 black strip (2½in x WOF) or fabric scraps

D: 1 red strip (2½in x WOF) or ¼yd

F: 6 seafoam green strips (2½in x WOF) or ½yd

Backing: 1½yd

Binding: 4 strips (2½in x WOF) or ½yd

Finished Size

43 x 26in

CUTTING FABRICS

Cut the shapes from fabrics A–D as described for the Area Rug, then cut the background pieces from fabric F as follows.

F Use 6 seafoam green strips (2½in x WOF)

F15 Cut 1 piece: 2½ x 19in; trim to create an isosceles trapezoid.

F13 Cut 2 pieces: 2½ x 16¾in; trim to create isosceles trapezoids.

F11 Cut 2 pieces: 2½ x 14½in; trim to create isosceles trapezoids.

FF4R & FF4L Cut 8 pieces: 2½ x 6½in; trim to create 4 right-leaning trapezoids and 4 left-leaning trapezoids.

FF3R & FF3L Cut 8 pieces: 2½ x 5¼in; trim to create 4 right-leaning trapezoids and 4 left-leaning trapezoids.

FF2R & FF2L Cut 8 pieces: 2½ x 4in; trim to create 4 right-leaning trapezoids and 4 left-leaning trapezoids.

F-3in Cut 2 pieces: 2½ x 3in.

PIECING AND QUILTING

Sew with a ¼in seam allowance, pressing the seams open.

EYES AND MOUTH
Same as for the Area Rug **(1–2)**.

MUZZLE
Construct 2 units – Sew A29, A31 and A33 together **(5)**.

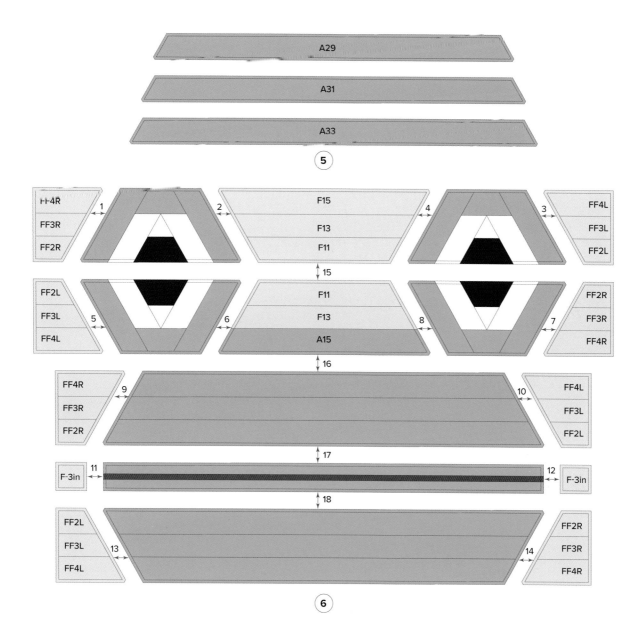

FINAL ASSEMBLY

In the following instructions, when piecing the right and left-leaning trapezoids, always align their 60° / 120° corners and sew to the side with the right angles.

Construct the background units – Sew F11, F13 and F15 together; sew F11, F13 and A15 together; sew FF4R, FF3R and FF2R together 4 times; sew FF4L, FF3L and FF2L together 4 times **(6)**.

Sew 2 pieces F-3in and all the units you made together in the order indicated **(6)**. Square up the finished top.

QUILTING AND BINDING

Make a quilt sandwich and quilt it as you like (see Useful Information). Bind your wall hanging using 4 strips 2½in x WOF (see Useful Information: Binding Rectangular Quilts). Add a few picture hanging strips to display the finished piece on the wall (see Additional Ideas: Wall Hanging).

2 PLACEMATS

Materials

B: 2 white strips (2½in x WOF) or ¼yd

C: 1 black strip (2½in x WOF) or fabric scraps

F: 8 seafoam green strips (2½in x WOF) or ¾yd

Backing: ½yd

Binding: 4 strips (2½in x WOF) or ½yd

Finished Size

20 x 11in

CUTTING FABRICS

B Use 2 white strips (2½in x WOF)

B3 Cut 8 pieces: 2½ x 5¼in; trim to create isosceles trapezoids.

C Use 1 black strip (2½in x WOF)

C-7½in Cut 1 piece: 2½ x 7½in and sub-cut into 2 rectangles 1 x 7½in.

F Use 8 seafoam green strips (2½in x WOF)

F7 Cut 2 pieces: 2½ x 9¾in; trim to create isosceles trapezoids.

FF7R & FF7L Cut 4 pieces: 2½ x 9¾in; trim to create 2 right-leaning trapezoids and 2 left-leaning trapezoids.

F6R & F6L Cut 2 pieces: 2½ x 8¾in; trim to create 1 right-leaning parallelogram and 1 left-leaning parallelogram.

FF6R & FF6L Cut 4 pieces: 2½ x 8¾in; trim to create 2 right-leaning trapezoids and 2 left-leaning trapezoids.

F5 Cut 4 pieces: 2½ x 7½in; trim to create isosceles trapezoids.

FF5R & FF5L Cut 4 pieces: 2½ x 7½in; trim to create 2 right-leaning trapezoids and 2 left-leaning trapezoids.

F4R & F4L Cut 4 pieces: 2½ x 6½in; trim to create 2 right-leaning parallelograms and 2 left-leaning parallelograms.

FF4R & FF4L Cut 4 pieces: 2½ x 6½in; trim to create 2 right-leaning trapezoids and 2 left-leaning trapezoids.

F3 Cut 2 pieces: 2½ x 5¼in; trim to create isosceles trapezoids.

FF3R & FF3L Cut 4 pieces: 2½ x 5¼in; trim to create 2 right-leaning trapezoids and 2 left-leaning trapezoids.

F-4in Cut 2 pieces: 2½ x 4in and sub-cut each piece into 2 rectangles 1 x 4in.

F2R & F2L Cut 2 pieces: 2½ x 4in; trim to create 1 right-leaning parallelogram and 1 left-leaning parallelogram.

FF2R & FF2L Cut 4 pieces: 2½ x 4in; trim to create 2 right-leaning trapezoids and 2 left-leaning trapezoids.

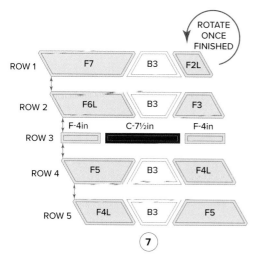

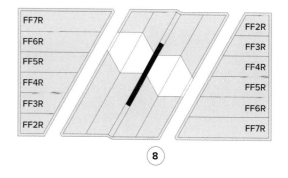

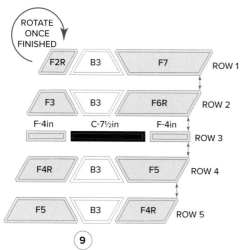

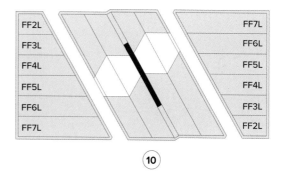

PIECING AND QUILTING

Sew with a ¼in seam allowance, pressing the seams open.

RIGHT-LEANING DRAGONFLY BLOCK

Construct 1 dragonfly unit – Sew F7, B3 and F2L together (Row 1); sew F6L, B3 and F3 together (Row 2); sew C-7½in and 2 pieces F-4in together (Row 3); sew F5, B3 and F4L together (Row 4); sew F4L, B3 and F5 together (Row 5); sew these 5 rows together **(7)**.

Construct 2 background units – Sew FF2R, FF3R, FF4R, FF5R, FF6R and FF7R together **(8)**.

Construct the block – Sew the background units on each side of the dragonfly unit and square up the block to 20½ x 11½in.

LEFT-LEANING DRAGONFLY BLOCK

Construct 1 dragonfly unit – Sew F7, B3 and F2R together (Row 1); sew F6R, B3 and F3 together (Row 2); sew C-7½in and 2 pieces F-4in together (Row 3); sew F5, B3 and F4R together (Row 4); sew F4R, B3 and F5 together (Row 5); sew these 5 rows together **(9)**.

Construct 2 background units – Sew FF2L, FF3L, FF4L, FF5L, FF6L and FF7L together **(10)**.

Construct the block – Sew the background units on each side of the dragonfly unit and square up the block to 20½ x 11½in.

QUILTING AND BINDING

Fold the backing fabric in half (with selvages together) and cut it along the fold. Make a quilt sandwich for each placemat. and quilt them as you like (see Useful Information). Bind each placemat using 2 strips 2½in x WOF (see Useful Information: Binding Rectangular Quilts).

QuilT

Materials

A: 20 green strips (2½in x WOF) or 1½yd

B: 6 white strips (2½in x WOF) or ½yd

C: 2 black strips (2½in x WOF) or ¼yd

D: 1 red strip (2½in x WOF) or ¼yd

E: 11 brown strips in various shades (2½in x WOF) or ¼yd of 4 different shades

F: 28 seafoam green strips (2½in x WOF) + 2yd or 4¼yd in total

Backing: 5yd

Binding: 9 strips (2½in x WOF) or ¾yd

Finished Size

71 x 82in

CUTTING FABRICS

Make 2 frog blocks as described for the Wall Hanging. Make 4 dragonfly blocks (2 right-facing and 2 left-facing) as described for the Placemats. Then cut the additional fabric F pieces as follows.

F Use additional seafoam green fabric (2yd)

Cut away selvages, then cut the following background pieces:

Horizontal Quilt Borders Cut 3 strips 5½in x LOF.

Horizontal Block Borders Cut 2 strips 6½in x LOF; sub-cut each strip into 2 borders 6½ x 27½in.

Sashing Cut 1 strip 7½in x LOF and sub-cut into 4 sashing pieces 7½ x 11½in.

PIECING AND QUILTING

Sew with a ¼in seam allowance unless otherwise indicated, pressing the seams open.

DRAGONFLY UNITS

Construct 2 units – Sew 2 horizontal block borders, 2 sashing pieces, 1 right-leaning dragonfly block and 1 left-leaning dragonfly block together in the order indicated **(11)**.

LOGS

Arrange 11 strips E, alternating the light, medium and dark strips, then sew them together along the long sides. From the finished piece, trim away selvages by placing your ruler perpendicular to the seams and sub-cut into 4 strips 8½in x LOF. Sew 2 of these units together along the short sides into a log and finish the second log in the same manner.

FINAL ASSEMBLY

Trim the logs to the width of your frog blocks and sew them to the bottom of each frog block in steps 1 and 2 **(12)**. Sew a dragonfly unit to the left edge of a frog block, and sew the remaining dragonfly unit to the right edge of the remaining frog block in steps 3 and 4 **(12)**. Referring to Useful Information: Borders, trim the edges of all horizontal quilt borders to the width of the finished units. Sew the units and borders together as indicated in steps 5–8 **(12)**.

QUILTING AND BINDING

Cut the backing fabric in half across WOF. Cut away selvages and sew 2 pieces together along the long sides with a ½in seam allowance; press the seam open. Make a quilt sandwich and quilt it as you like (see Useful Information). Bind your quilt using 9 strips 2½in x WOF (see Useful Information: Binding Rectangular Quilts).

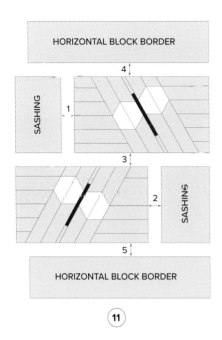

⑪

EXTRAS

PILLOWCASES

To make 2 pillowcases, you will need fabric strips required for the placemats plus additional background fabric, and fabrics for backing and binding. To complete the tops, simply make a right-leaning dragonfly block and a left-leaning dragonfly block, then add borders from your background fabric to make them square. Finish your pillowcases as described in Additional Ideas: Pillowcase.

BANNER

You will need 4 strips B, 2 strips C, 12 strips F + ¼yd of fabric F, and fabrics for backing and binding. Construct 3 left-leaning dragonfly flag units, referring to Rows 1–5 of placemat unit diagram **(7)** and 3 right-leaning dragonfly flag units, referring to Rows 1–5 of placemat unit diagram **(9)**. From fabric F, cut 1 strip 8in x WOF and sub-cut into 6 rectangles 4½ x 8in. Cut 3 of these rectangles diagonally from the upper right to the bottom left corner, and cut the remaining 3 rectangles in the mirrored direction. Sew the first set of half-rectangles to the right-leaning dragonflies **(13)** and sew the remaining set of half-rectangles to the left-leaning dragonflies **(14)**. Square up each flag unit. Finish the banner as described in Additional Ideas: Banner.

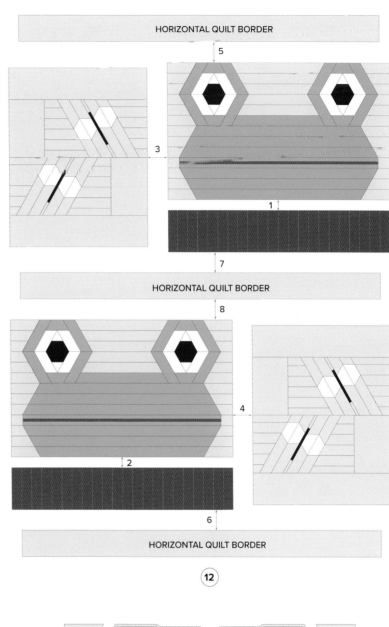

⑫

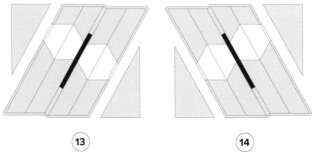

⑬ ⑭

ADDITIONAL IDEAS

Create even more adorable projects using motifs from different animal patterns. You can make banners, pillows, wall hangings, or incorporate motifs into other sewing projects. Why not mix and match blocks from different animals to create your own animal quilts? Make a cat and dog quilt with paw prints from the bear pattern or use the fox and raccoon blocks for a woodland theme quilt. Improvising is also great for using up your fabric scraps to make a backing with coordinating blocks from the quilt. Or incorporate old jeans into your patchwork project to help the planet while being creative. The possibilities are endless.

MIX 'N' MATCH QUILTS

Here are a few ideas to get you started on designing even more animal-inspired quilt designs, including making an improv backing to match your animal theme.

CAT AND DOG QUILT (73 x 80in)

Make 1 cat block, 1 dog block and 2 sets of paw print blocks from the bear quilt. Cut additional background pieces as shown in the diagram and sew everything together **(1)**.

FOX AND RACCOON QUILT (70 x 80in)

Make 1 fox block, 1 raccoon block and 2 forest borders from the fox quilt. Cut additional background pieces as shown in the diagram and sew everything together **(2)**

IMPROV BACKING (65 x 74in)

When planning an improv backing, it should always be 2–3in longer and wider than your quilt top on each side*. For instance, if the bear quilt is 61 x 70in, your backing should be at least 65 x 74in. Make 3 left-facing and 2 right-facing paw blocks from the bear quilt. Cut additional background pieces as shown in the diagram and sew everything together **(3)**.

*Note: If you plan to have your quilt longarm quilted, your improv backing should be 4–5in longer and wider than your quilt top on each side.

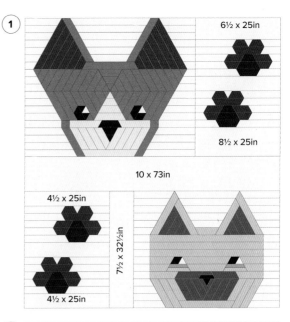

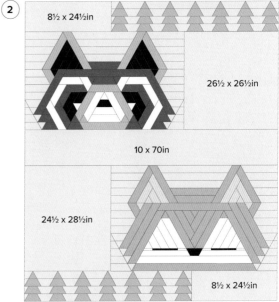

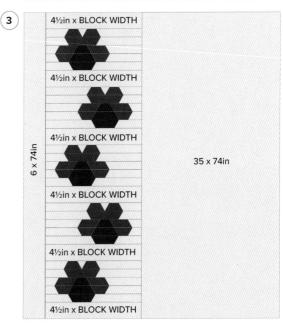

BANNER

A banner is a set of colorful flags joined together; it is also known as bunting. It will make a fun coordinating addition to your room.

Begin by picking a motif from your quilt and construct a few flags using fabric scraps from your projects. Each animal theme has a hint on which motifs you can use, or you can choose your own.

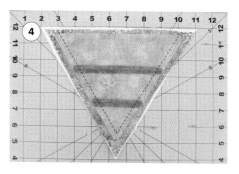

For each flag, cut a piece of backing and batting slightly larger than your flag unit. With the right sides of the flag unit and backing fabric together, position them on top of the batting. Sew along the side edges of the flag unit with a ¼in seam allowance, leaving the top edge open **(4)**. Cut away the excess backing and batting on each side to the size of the flag unit, but don't trim the top edge yet. Snip away the extra fabric around the convex corners to reduce bulk, being careful not to cut through the stitches **(5)**.

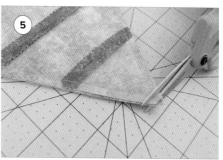

Insert your fingers between the front and back fabric layers and turn each flag right side out through the top opening so the batting is now in between the two fabric layers. Use a point turner to push out the corners gently. Press the side edges with a hot iron just slightly towards the backing, approximately ⅛in.

Topstitch or edgestitch along the pressed sides on the front of the flags and quilt them as you like (see Useful Information: Quilting). Trim away the excess fabric on the top edge of the flags.

The flags are now joined by sewing them onto a length of bias tape to make the banner. You can use precut bias tape or make your own double-fold bias tape as follows. Cut 2in wide strips at a 45° angle; sew these strips together into a 80–90in strip. Using a bias maker, fold and press the edges so they meet in the center, then fold the strip in half along the center and press again.

Position the flags along the bias tape, spacing them evenly from the center out and leaving the sides longer for ties. You can place the flags next to each other or leave a 1–3in space between them. Tuck the raw edge of the flags in between the layers of the bias tape and use pins to hold them in place **(6)**.

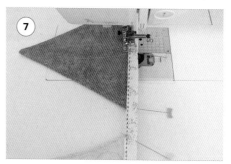

Trim and fold in the raw ends of the bias tape and pin them in place. Topstitch from end to end along the tape, attaching the flags and removing the pins as you sew **(7)**.

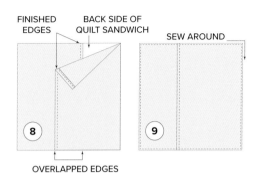

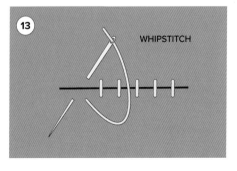

PILLOWCASE

It's easy to make a coordinating pillowcase for your animal quilt using elements from the quilt design. A simple envelope pillowcase is easy to adapt to different finished sizes depending on the motifs selected.

To Make the Front
— Make a small block from your quilt pattern. Add background fabric to the top and bottom edges or trim the sides to the desired size. The finished block should be about 1in larger vertically and horizontally than your pillow insert. Make a quilt sandwich and quilt it as you like (see Useful Information). Square up the finished front to the size of the pillow insert, adding ¼in to each side for seam allowances.

To Make the Back
— Cut 2 identical fabric pieces measuring as follows: Height = the height of the front cover; Width = ½ of the front cover width + 3½in for overlap. Finish one raw edge vertically on each piece: fold the raw edge to the wrong side by ⅜in and press; fold the hem over again, press then stitch closely along the first fold.

Final Assembly
— Lay the front right side facing down and place the hemmed backing fabric rectangles on top with right sides facing up, so that the finished edges overlap in the center and the raw edges of the back align with the edges of the front **(8)**. Pin and sew around with a ¼in seam allowance **(9)**. Bind your pillowcase using 2½in strips (see Useful Information: Binding Rectangular Quilts).

NON-SLIP RUG BACKING

A removable rug backing is ideal for quilted rugs as you can then wash and dry them separately, avoiding the risk of melting the backing material and preventing the uneven shrinkage of the two elements.

Cut a rectangle from the rug pad, which usually comes on a roll, to the size of your quilted rug; it should cover the area without going over the edges **(10)**. You can simply place the backing under your rug to hold it in place and prevent it from sliding, but if you wish, you can attach the corners of the backing to the rug for extra security using adhesive hook-and-loop tape. Cut 4 pieces of hook-and-loop tape about 3in long. Remove the paper liner from the hook side of the tape and stick each piece to a corner of the pad. Recenter the pad on the reverse of the rug, with the taped corners facing down. Carefully remove the paper liner from the loop side of each piece of the tape in turn and press firmly to attach to the rug **(11)**. Remove the grip, separating the hooks and loops gently, and whipstitch around the loop tape onto the backing fabric of the rug **(12–13)**, being careful not to stitch through to the front of the quilt. There's no need to sew the hook tape to the backing, but you could add a few drops of fabric glue for extra security and let it dry. Remove the backing when you need to wash the rug.

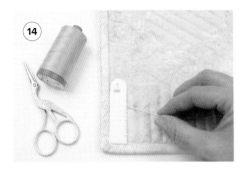

WALL HANGING

Use 6 pairs of damage-free wall hanging strips to display your hanging on the wall. Position and stick the first strip from each pair to the back of your quilt – 1 strip in each corner and 2 strips along the top edge between the corners. The bottom corners are optional, but they will keep the edges nice and straight. Whipstitch **(13)** around each strip onto the backing **(14)**. Pair up the remaining strips with the strips on your quilt and press each pair together until they click. Remove the paper liner and follow the manufacturer's instructions to attach your quilt to the wall. To ensure the adhesive holds, gently remove the quilt and press each strip to the wall firmly for 30 seconds. Let the strips dry in position on the wall for an hour before re-hanging your quilt **(15)**.

As an option, you can attach the wall hanging strips to decorative clips or clothespins and then attach them to the wall in a horizontal row. This way you do not need to sew the strips to the quilt. Simply use the clips to hold your quilt and change your quilt display from time to time **(16)**.

UPCYCLING

Upcycling is a creative way of honoring pre-loved clothing. It also reduces our environmental footprint by saving the planet from waste. Rugs made from denim strips look fantastic and you can even combine denim with colorful fabric strips in the background **(17)**.

To prepare denim strips, simply cut away the waist band, pockets and all seams from your old jeans, then press the back and front sides. Cut the denim into 2½in strips lengthwise. Avoid using very stretchy jeans as elastic material may become distorted while sewing.

Sew with a ¼in seam allowance, pressing the seams open or to the side if it helps to reduce bulk. I use 50wt cotton thread with an 80/12 topstitch needle (the same size used for quilting cotton). Aurifil Arctic Sky (2612) thread blends in nicely with different shades of denim, and works for both piecing and quilting.

Use up batting leftovers from the quilts to make rugs. Position the pieces of batting with the long edges side by side and piece them together with the widest zig-zag stitch on your sewing machine.

USEFUL INFORMATION

This section features special terminology used in the book, as well as all the essential techniques and advice on finishing your projects, such as adding borders, making a quilt sandwich, quilting, and various binding techniques.

COMMON TERMS

Basting – A technique that allows you to hold three layers of a quilt sandwich together using curved pins or basting spray.

Basting stitch – The longest straight stitch on your sewing machine.

Batting (wadding) – An insulation layer of soft fibers between the quilt top and the quilt backing.

Bias grain – The grain on woven fabric that runs in both diagonal directions at a 45° angle.

Binding – A long strip of double-folded fabric that covers the raw edges of a quilt.

Borders – Strips of fabric sewn to the edges of a quilt.

Chain-piecing – Sewing unit after unit without cutting the thread in between each set.

Corner trimmer – An acrylic or paper template for trimming corners.

Cross grain – The grain on woven fabric that runs across the width of the fabric from selvage to selvage.

Dog-ears – Fabric points that stick out past the seam allowance if not trimmed before piecing.

Edgestitch – A decorative straight stitch, sewn ⅛in away from the edge on the front side.

Free motion quilting – A special quilting technique that allows you to move a quilt sandwich in all directions without using feed-dogs on a domestic sewing machine, or hover over the surface of your quilt with a longarm machine.

In – Inch(es), an imperial unit of measurement.

Jelly Roll – A bundle of precut fabric strips that measure 2½in x WOF.

LOF – Length of fabric.

Longarm quilting – Joining multiple layers of fabric into a quilt using a special sewing machine with a large throat space.

Mm – Millimeter(s), a metric unit of measurement, used to reflect standard markings on suggested equipments.

Masking tape – A thin and easy-to-tear adhesive paper.

Piecing – Sewing fabric pieces together to form a block or a quilt.

Pressing – A method of lifting the hot iron up and down to ensure that seams are smooth and flat.

Ruler foot – A special foot with a raised edge for quilting along the edge of special templates on a sewing or quilting machine.

Quilting – Joining multiple layers of fabric together using a sewing or quilting machine, or by hand.

Quilt sandwich – Three layers of a quilt made up of the quilt top, the batting and the quilt backing.

Selvage – A tightly woven edge of fabric that protects it from fraying and unraveling.

Setting seams – Pressing the seams flat as they were sewn before pressing them open or to the side.

Stitch-in-the-ditch – Sewing along the existing seam.

Straight grain – The grain on woven fabric that runs parallel to the selvages of the fabric.

Squaring up – Making the corners cut square at a 90° angle, and the sides cut straight.

Topstitch – A decorative straight stitch, sewn ¼in away from the edge on the front side.

Walking foot – A special foot for quilting on a sewing machine that evenly feeds several layers of fabric through the machine.

WOF – Width of fabric.

Yd – Yard(s), an imperial unit of measurement.

BORDERS

Borders are strips of fabric or pieced units sewn to the edges of a quilt. Measuring and adding borders properly will ensure the square appearance of your quilt, without waves around the edges.

To prepare horizontal borders, measure your quilt horizontally across the center. To prepare vertical borders, measure your quilt vertically across the center. Instead of using a measuring tape, you can simply lay your borders across the center of the quilt and trim them in that position. Trim borders to the exact measurements, then pin them evenly across the edges from side to side and sew (1–2). Never sew the borders without measuring your quilt first.

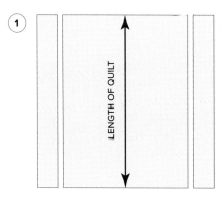

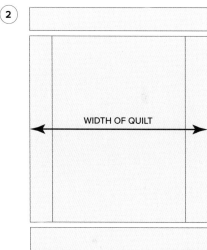

QUILT SANDWICH

Making a quilt sandwich is a traditional method for preparing your fabric layers and batting for quilting. Use this method if making a quilt or a wall hanging, but if making an area rug, refer to Rug Without Binding.

Preparing the Backing and Batting — Once your quilt top is finished, trim your backing fabric and batting so that they are longer and wider than your quilt top by 2–3in on each side (or 4–6in total). If you are planning to quilt your project on a longarm machine, the backing and batting should be 4–5in longer and wider on each side (or 8–10in total). Iron your backing fabric and, if you have had to piece the backing (where the width of the project is greater than the WOF), press seams open.

Select Your Basting Tools — I use the size-1 curved basting pins (approximately 1in long) to hold my quilt layers together. If you prefer to spray-baste, follow the manufacturer's instructions and test prior to using it on a quilt. There is nothing worse than a gummed up needle and an uncooperative sewing machine!

Layer the Quilt Sandwich — Lay your backing fabric on the floor or a large table with the wrong side facing up. Use masking tape to secure the corners and the edges around the perimeter (3). Lay out the batting on top of the backing fabric, flattening wrinkles carefully without stretching it. Lay the quilt top on the batting with the right side facing up.

Pin-basting — To secure all three layers of your quilt sandwich together, place curved basting pins every 4–6in. Use a pin fastening tool (or a teaspoon) to easily and safely raise the sharp pin into the closure. Once securely pinned, remove the masking tape from the backing and proceed to quilting (see Quilting).

Finishing — Once quilted, trim away the excess batting and backing then bind your quilt (see Straight and Cross Grain Binding or Bias Binding).

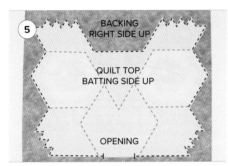

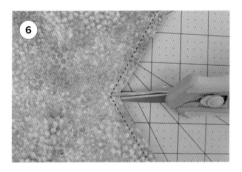

RUG WITHOUT BINDING

Finishing quilts without a binding is a non-traditional method that provides an alternative to the complexity of binding rugs with irregular edges. You will need fabric snips for clipping corners and a point turner for turning every point perfectly.

Preparing the Top – Lay your finished quilt top right side up onto a piece of batting and pin baste to hold the two layers together. Stitch-in-the-ditch around the main intersections to stabilize the fabrics **(4)**; do not remove basting pins. Sew a basting stitch all the way around the quilt top, approximately ⅛in away from the edge. Trim away the excess batting.

Adding the Backing Layer – Lay the backing fabric down with the right side facing up and place the quilt top on top of it with the batting side facing up. Pin to secure, then sew around the edge of the quilt top with a ¼in seam allowance, leaving a 6–8in opening at the bottom edge for turning **(5)**. Trim away the excess backing fabric. Clip the concave corners to release tension **(6)** and trim away the convex corners to reduce bulk **(7)**, being careful not to cut through the stitches. For curved edges, clip a few notches around the curves.

Finishing – Turn your rug right side out through the opening, using a point turner to push out the corners gently. Press the edges around the entire rug just slightly towards the backing, approximately ¹⁄₁₆in. Topstitch or edgestitch around the front side. Flatten out your project and use the basting pins, still in place on the quilt top, to catch the backing fabric to hold all three layers together. Quilt as you like (see Quilting). If needed, press around the edges gently on the back.

QUILTING

When it comes to quilting, the only limit to what you can create with your sewing machine is your imagination. Use a walking foot for any straight and curved lines, a darning foot for freemotion quilting, or quilt with special templates and a ruler foot. Pick designs that you feel comfortable stitching and quilt them as you see fit into your project. You can create an all-over-design using the same pattern and thread for the entire project, or customize sections of your quilt using different patterns and matching threads.

To keep your quilting designs neat, use masking tape to mark your lines and stitch just a touch away from the tape. You can also use marking tools, but be sure to test them on a piece of fabric before using them on your quilt. Here are a few beginner-friendly designs you can choose from. If you are new to quilting, you can practice them with a pen on paper before stitching on fabric.

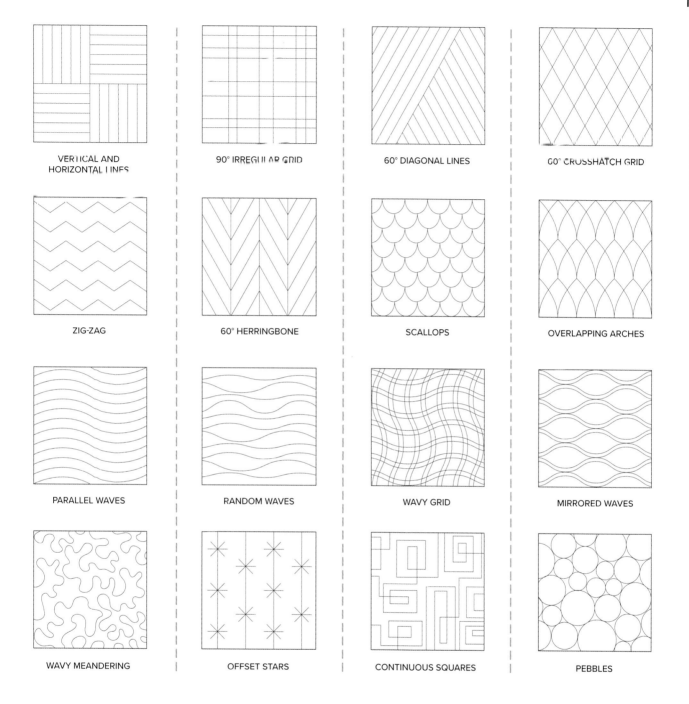

VERTICAL AND
HORIZONTAL LINES

90° IRREGULAR GRID

60° DIAGONAL LINES

60° CROSSHATCH GRID

ZIG-ZAG

60° HERRINGBONE

SCALLOPS

OVERLAPPING ARCHES

PARALLEL WAVES

RANDOM WAVES

WAVY GRID

MIRRORED WAVES

WAVY MEANDERING

OFFSET STARS

CONTINUOUS SQUARES

PEBBLES

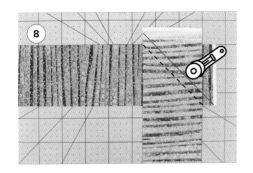

STRAIGHT AND CROSS GRAIN BINDING

For finishing quilts with straight edges.

Cutting Strips – Cross grain binding strips are cut across the fabric width from selvage to selvage (2½in x WOF), or you can use precut fabric strips. Straight grain binding strips are cut along the fabric length and have the least stretch (2½in x LOF).

Making Binding – With the right sides together, overlap 2 binding strips perpendicularly. Pin and sew the strips together diagonally from the upper-left corner to the bottom-right corner. Repeat sewing strips to the indicated length. Trim away the excess fabric and dog-ears, leaving ¼in for seam allowance **(8)**. Press all seams open, then fold your binding strip in half lengthwise and press.

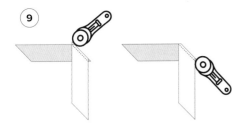

BIAS BINDING

Bias binding is absolutely essential for finishing curved edges. It's very flexible and is easy to maneuver around the curved edges without tightening them up.

Cutting Strips – Use markings on the ruler or your cutting mat to make the first cut at a 45° angle. You can also fold the fabric diagonally to determine your first diagonal line. Align the 2½in mark of the ruler with the bias edge and cut your first strip. Continue cutting 2½in bias strips until you have enough strips for the required length.

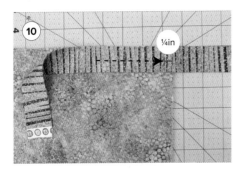

Making Binding – Match the edges of the strips based on the slanting direction. Holding the strips perpendicular, with the right sides together, sew them along the diagonal edge with a ¼in seam allowance. Trim the dog-ears then press the seam open **(9)**. Fold the long bias strip in half lengthwise and press.

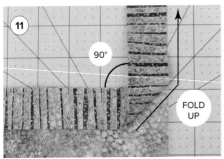

BINDING RECTANGULAR QUILTS

This technique is used for binding quilts, rectangular placemats, pillowcases and wall hangings using a straight or cross grain binding (see Straight and Cross Grain Binding). The binding can be finished by sewing machine or by hand, as you choose.

To Begin – Line up the raw edges of the binding with the quilt edge, on the back if finishing by sewing machine or on the front if finishing by hand. Leaving an end of 6–8in, begin sewing at least a few inches away from the corner.

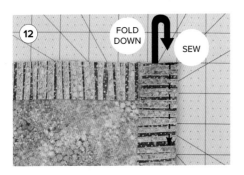

Sewing Corners — Sew towards the corner with a ¼in seam allowance and stop ¼in away from the edge **(10)**. Backstitch, cut off the thread and rotate your quilt to sew the next edge. Fold the binding strip up, creating a continuous straight edge with the quilt on the right and a 90° corner between the binding edges **(11)**. Fold the binding strip down and match the raw edges with the quilt edge; sew from the top edge down **(12)**. Repeat around the other corners.

Joining Binding Ends — Stop 6–10in before your starting point (this space may vary depending on the size of your project). Trim the ends, overlapping them in the center by 2½in, which is the width of the unfolded binding strip **(13)**. Holding the ends perpendicularly with right sides together, sew them with a diagonal seam from corner to corner **(14)**. Trim away the excess fabric leaving a ¼in seam allowance and finger-press the seam open **(15)**. Sew the remaining part of the binding to the quilt.

Finishing Binding by Sewing Machine — Fold the binding to the front of the quilt and sew towards the corner. At the corner, fold the binding over to one side then back to the center to form a nice corner; you can use pins or wonder-clips to keep your folded binding in place. Sew until the needle hits the folded edge of the corner **(16)**. Stop with the needle down and pivot. Continue sewing around the edge, passing all corners in the same manner.

Finishing Binding by Hand — Fold the binding to the back of the quilt and sew with ladder stitch **(17)**, folding the corners in the same manner as for Finishing Binding By Sewing Machine.

BINDING CURVED EDGES

This technique is used in some area rugs with curved edges. It's important to use bias binding for curved edges (see Bias Binding). Do not use a straight or cross grain binding as they will not lay flat around the curves. Line up the raw edges of the binding with the quilt edge on the back (or on the front if you plan to finish binding by hand). Begin sewing from any point, except corners if there are any. Do not stretch your binding strip or quilt when sewing around the curves. If there are irregular corners along the way, refer to Binding 120° Corners, Binding 60° Corners and Binding Concave Corners. Join the binding ends, then finish binding on the front side by machine or on the back side by hand as described for Binding Rectangular Quilts.

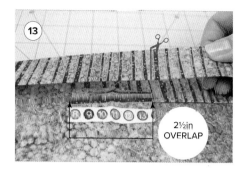

13 — 2½in OVERLAP

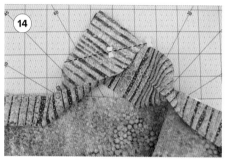

14

15

16

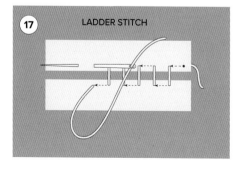

17 — LADDER STITCH

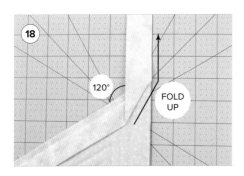

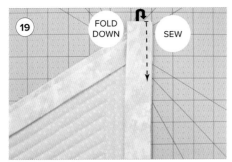

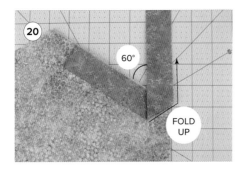

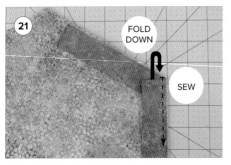

BINDING 60° CORNERS

When sewing binding around 60° corners, stop at the center of the corner, ¼in away from the edge. Backstitch, cut off the thread and rotate your quilt to sew the next edge. Fold the binding strip up, creating a continuous straight edge with the quilt on the right and a 120° corner between the binding edges **(18)**. Fold the binding strip down and match the raw edges with the quilt edge; sew from the top edge down **(19)**.

Finish binding on the front side by machine or on the back side by hand. At the corners, fold the binding over to one side then back to the center to form a nice corner. Sew until the needle hits the folded edge of the corner, stop with the needle down and pivot. Continue sewing around the edge.

BINDING 120° CORNERS

When sewing binding around 120° corners, stop at the center of the corner, ¼in away from the edge. Backstitch, cut off the thread and rotate your quilt to sew the next edge. Fold the binding strip up, creating a continuous straight edge with the quilt on the right and a 60° corner between the binding edges **(20)**. Fold the binding strip down and match the raw edges with the quilt edge; sew from the top edge down **(21)**.

Finish binding on the front side by machine or on the back side by hand. At the corners, fold the binding over to one side then back to the center to form a nice corner. Sew until the needle hits the folded edge of the corner, stop with the needle down and pivot. Continue sewing around the edge.

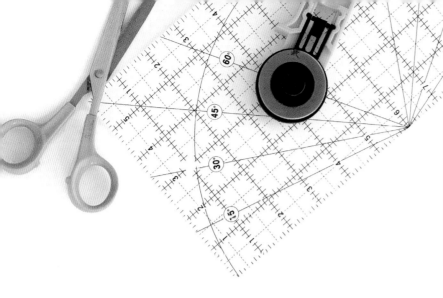

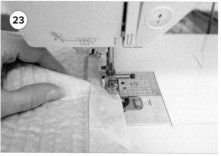

BINDING CONCAVE CORNERS

When sewing binding around concave corners, stop at the center of the corner with the needle down **(22)**. Pinch the fabric on the left to straighten out the right edge **(23)**. It will keep your stitching path straight and help you pass the concave corner smoothly. Continue sewing around the edge.

Once finished, cut out a notch in the concave corners of the binding to reduce bulk, being very careful not to cut through the stitches. Pinch the excess fabric in the corner so that the binding is flat **(24)**. Fold the binding strip to the front of the quilt if sewing by machine or to the back if sewing by hand, pin and sew around the edge **(25)**.

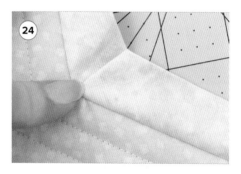

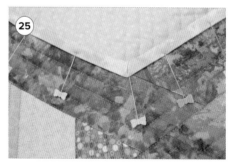

Happy Crafting!

ABOUT THE AUTHOR

Hi! I am a Canadian fiber artist, pattern designer and author. I was born and raised in the beautiful city of Zaporizhzhia, located on the Dnieper River in southeastern Ukraine. As a child of textile engineers, I grew up in a home packed with fabrics, threads, yarns and books. I never missed an opportunity to create, either with my parents, grandparents, or in school. Needle-crafting has always felt natural to me.

I started sewing by hand when I was very young and I purchased my own sewing machine at the age of 12. Later on, I learned how to measure and design my own garments. I made my first scrap quilt when I was a teenager, but the real love for quilting came later in life. In 2015, I stumbled upon a group of quilters at the Fergus Scottish Festival. Noticing my enthusiasm, the quilting crew invited me to the frame with a beautiful quilt and let me quilt a portion of it. That was the beginning of my quilting journey.

I enjoy sharing my passion for fiber art through my designs inspired by animals and nature. My happy place is where fabric and yarn meet fun!

I hope you enjoy making animal quilts from this book as much as I enjoyed designing them. If you also like crocheting, you can check out my previous books from the animal series – *Crochet Animal Rugs*, *Crochet Animal Slippers*, and *Crochet Animal Blankets and Blocks*.

THANKS

I would like to thank Northcott for providing their gorgeous quilting fabrics for the projects in this book, and thanks to Aurifil threads for supplying their high quality cotton thread for sewing and quilting these projects. A very special thank you goes out to my team members for testing and proofreading patterns in this book — Cheryl McNichols, Lenore Cartlidge, Linda McLaren, Ryan Nicole Hazeltine, Helen Hamilton, Brenda Byrum and Cynthia Fuller. Also, big thanks to my tech editor Teresa Kent of Come Stitch With Me for providing great services and helping me over the years.

SUPPLIES

Fabrics
Northcott — Northcott.com
Patrick Lose — Patricklose.com

Thread
Aurifil — Aurifil.com

Batting
Hobbs — HobbsBatting.com
Alberta Batting Company — AlbertaBattingCompany.com

Fabric Shops
Canada — Dinkydoo.com
USA — Missouriquiltco.com
Worldwide — Quiltinghub.com

Additional Supplies
Canada — Fabricland.ca
USA — Joann.com
Worldwide — Amazon.com

INDEX

A DAVID AND CHARLES BOOK
© David and Charles, Ltd 2024

David and Charles is an imprint of David and Charles, Ltd
Suite A, Tourism House, Pynes Hill, Exeter, EX2 5WS

Text and Designs © IraRott Inc. 2024
Layout and Photography © David and Charles, Ltd 2024

First published in the UK and USA in 2024

A catalogue record for this book is
available from the British Library.

ISBN-13: 9781446310588 paperback
ISBN-13: 9781446312001 EPUB
ISBN-13: 9781446311899 PDF

This book has been printed on paper from approved
suppliers and made from pulp from sustainable sources.

FSC
www.fsc.org
MIX
Paper from
responsible sources
FSC® C012521

Printed in China through Asia Pacific Offset for:
David and Charles, Ltd
Suite A, Tourism House, Pynes Hill, Exeter, EX2 5WS

10 9 8 7 6 5 4 3 2 1

Publishing Director: Ame Verso
Senior Commissioning Editor: Sarah Callard
Managing Editor: Jeni Chown
Editor: Victoria Allen
Project Editor: Cheryl Brown
Head of Design: Anna Wade
Designer: Jess Pearson, Marieclare
Mayne and Lee-May Lim
Pre-press Designer: Susan Reansbury
Art Direction: Prudence Rogers
Photography: Jason Jenkins
Production Manager: Beverley Richardson

David and Charles publishes high-quality
books on a wide range of subjects. For more
information visit www.davidandcharles.com.

Share your makes with us on social media using
#dandcbooks and follow us on Facebook and
Instagram by searching for @dandcbooks.

Full-size printable versions of the templates are
available to download from the Bookmarked Hub: www.
bookmarkedhub.com. Search for this book by the title
or ISBN: the files can be found under 'Book Extras'.
Membership of the Bookmarked online community is free.

Layout of the digital edition of this book may vary
depending on reader hardware and display settings.